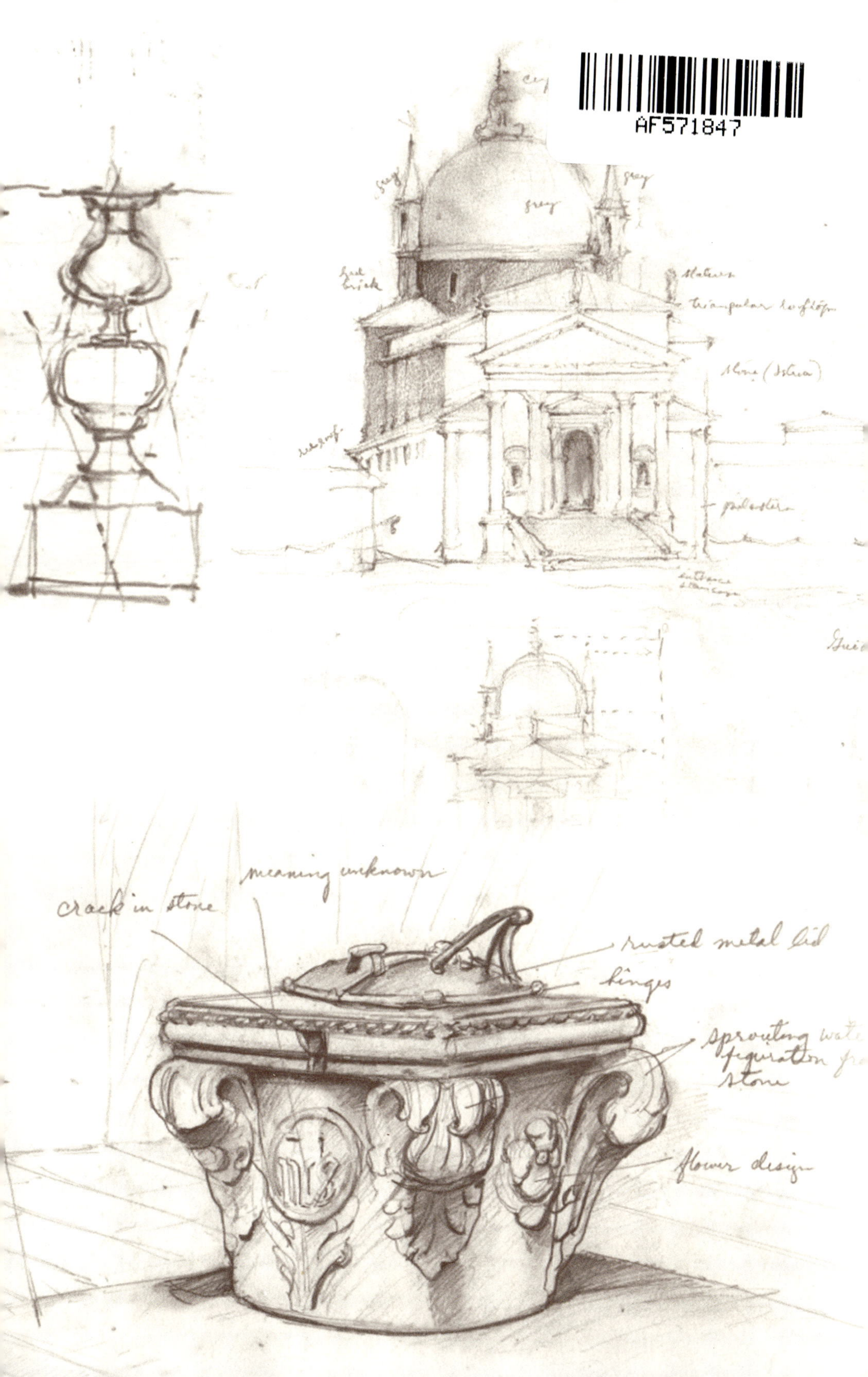
grey
grey
grey
statues
triangular rooftop
pilasters
meaning unknown
crack in stone
rusted metal lid
hinges
flower design

12/2018

Dear Mom and Dad:

Because of your love of its beauty –

Merry Christmas!

Love, Doro

AN ARTIST IN VENICE

BY

ADAM VAN DOREN

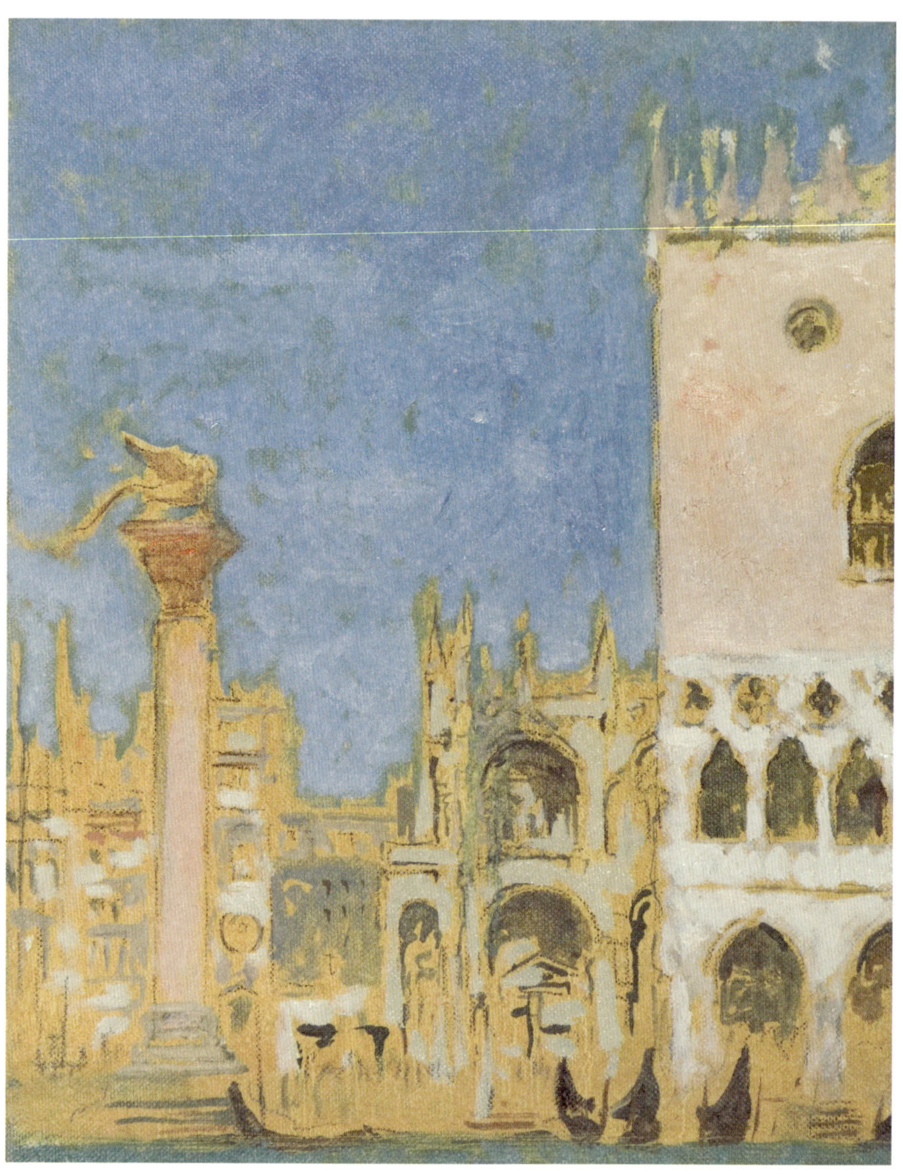

Vignette of San Marco, *2010*

"The Piazza also acts as a natural portal to Venice, welcoming its visitors like conquering heroes of yore."

AN ARTIST IN VENICE

BY

ADAM VAN DOREN

With a Preface

by Theodore K. Rabb

&

a Foreword by

Simon Winchester

DAVID R. GODINE · PUBLISHER

BOSTON

First published in 2013 by
DAVID R. GODINE · PUBLISHER
Post Office Box 450
Jaffrey, New Hampshire 03452
www.godine.com

Map by Nick Springer

Library of Congress Cataloging-in-Publication Data
Van Doren, Adam, 1962–
An Artist in Venice / By Adam Van Doren ; With a Preface by Theodore K. Rabb ; A Foreword by Simon Winchester.
— First.
p. cm.
Includes bibliographical references.
ISBN 978-1-56792-454-1 (alk. paper)
1. Van Doren, Adam, 1962– —Themes, motives. 2. Venice (Italy)—In art. I. Title.
ND1839.V34A4 2012
759.13—dc23
2011046652

FIRST EDITION
PRINTED IN CHINA

It was
the inevitable
destiny of Venice
to be painted . . . and
painted with
passion.

Henry James

TABLE OF CONTENTS

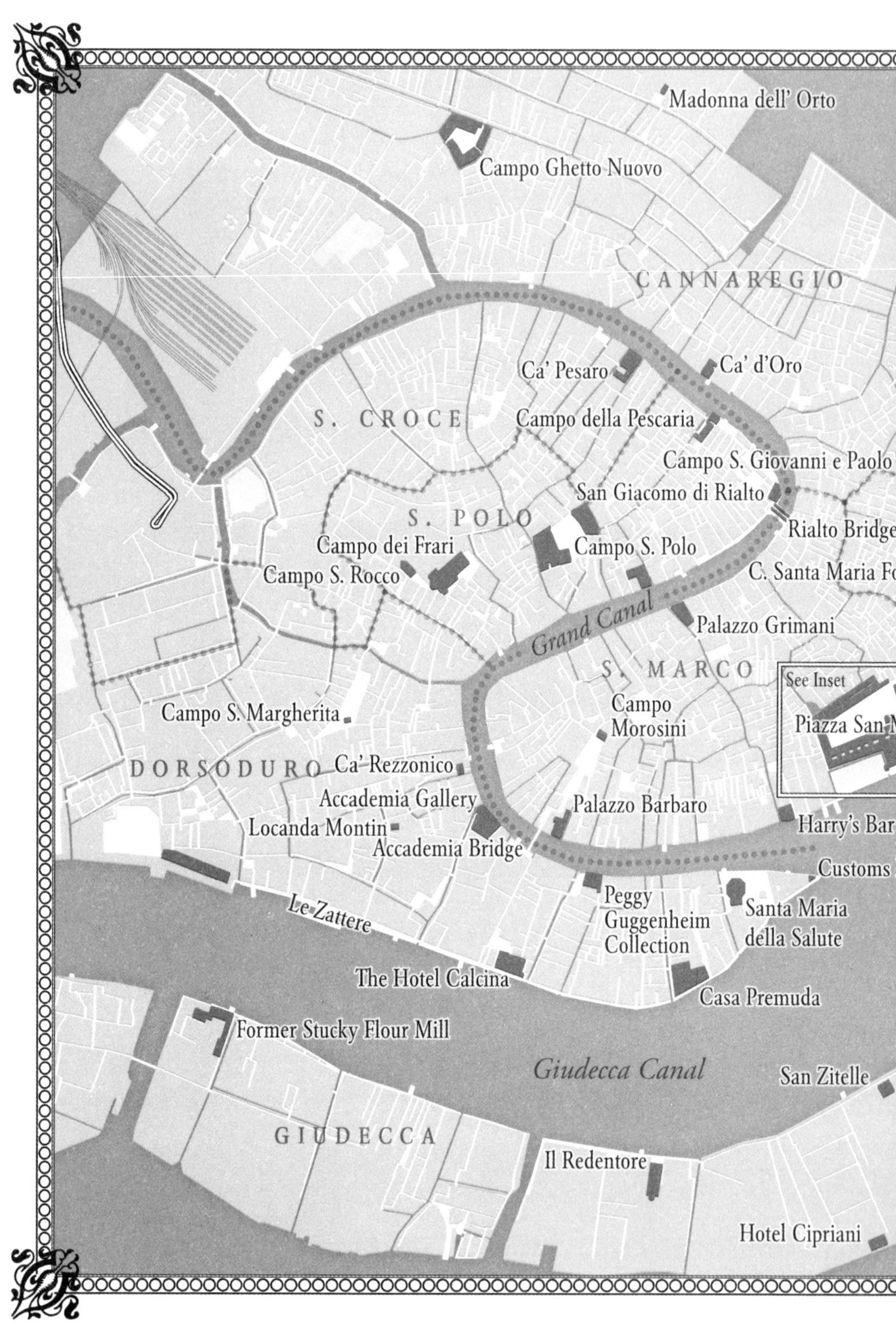
Madonna dell' Orto
Campo Ghetto Nuovo
CANNAREGIO
Ca' Pesaro
Ca' d'Oro
S. CROCE
Campo della Pescaria
Campo S. Giovanni e Paolo
San Giacomo di Rialto
S. POLO
Rialto Bridge
Campo dei Frari
Campo S. Polo
Campo S. Rocco
Palazzo Grimani
Grand Canal
S. MARCO
See Inset
Campo S. Margherita
Campo Morosini
DORSODURO
Ca' Rezzonico
Accademia Gallery
Palazzo Barbaro
Locanda Montin
Accademia Bridge
Harry's Bar
Le Zattere
Peggy Guggenheim Collection
Santa Maria della Salute
The Hotel Calcina
Casa Premuda
Former Stucky Flour Mill
Giudecca Canal
San Zitelle
GIUDECCA
Il Redentore
Hotel Cipriani

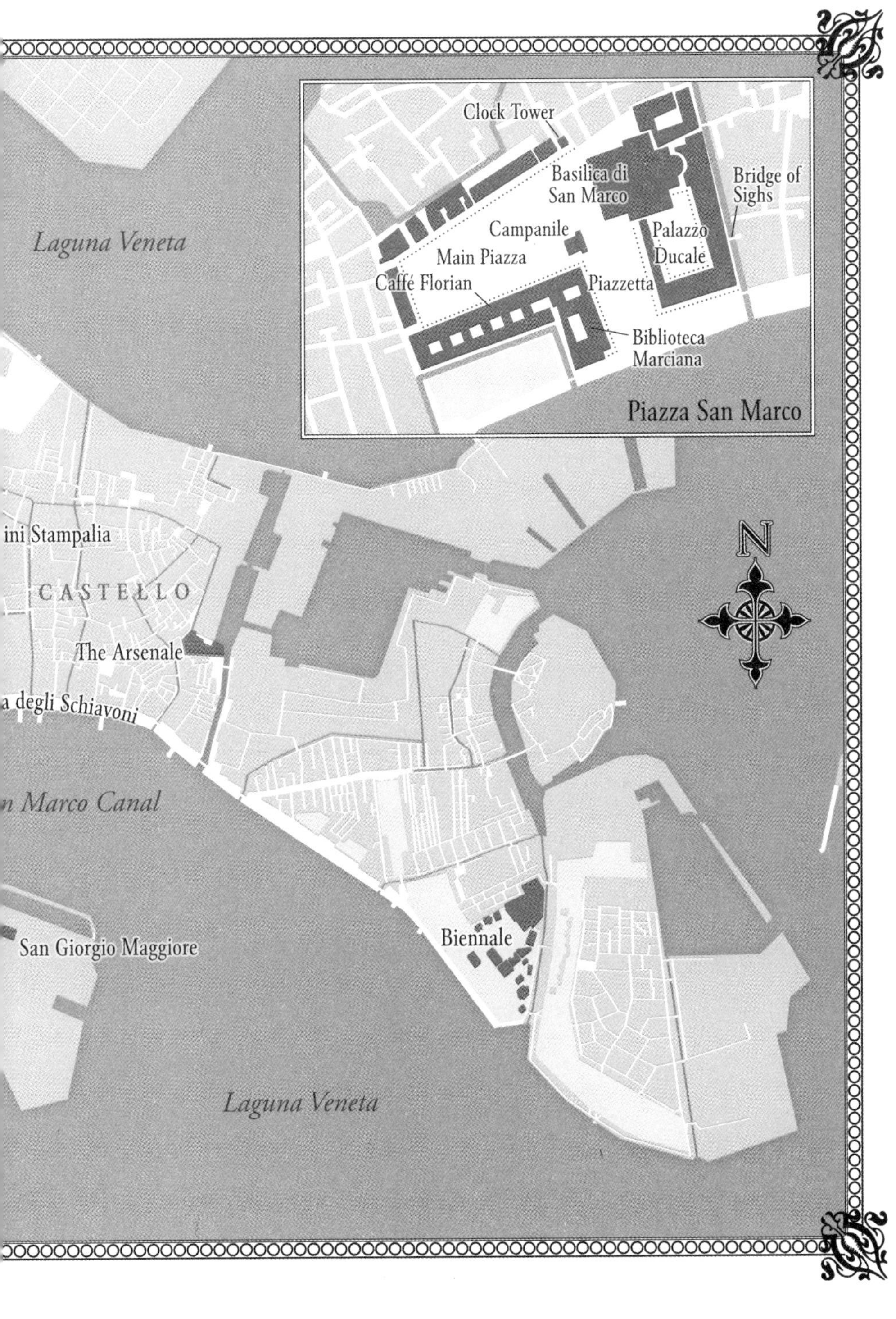
Clock Tower
Basilica di San Marco
Bridge of Sighs
Campanile
Main Piazza
Palazzo Ducale
Caffé Florian
Piazzetta
Biblioteca Marciana
Piazza San Marco
Laguna Veneta
N
ini Stampalia
CASTELLO
The Arsenale
a degli Schiavoni
n Marco Canal
San Giorgio Maggiore
Biennale
Laguna Veneta

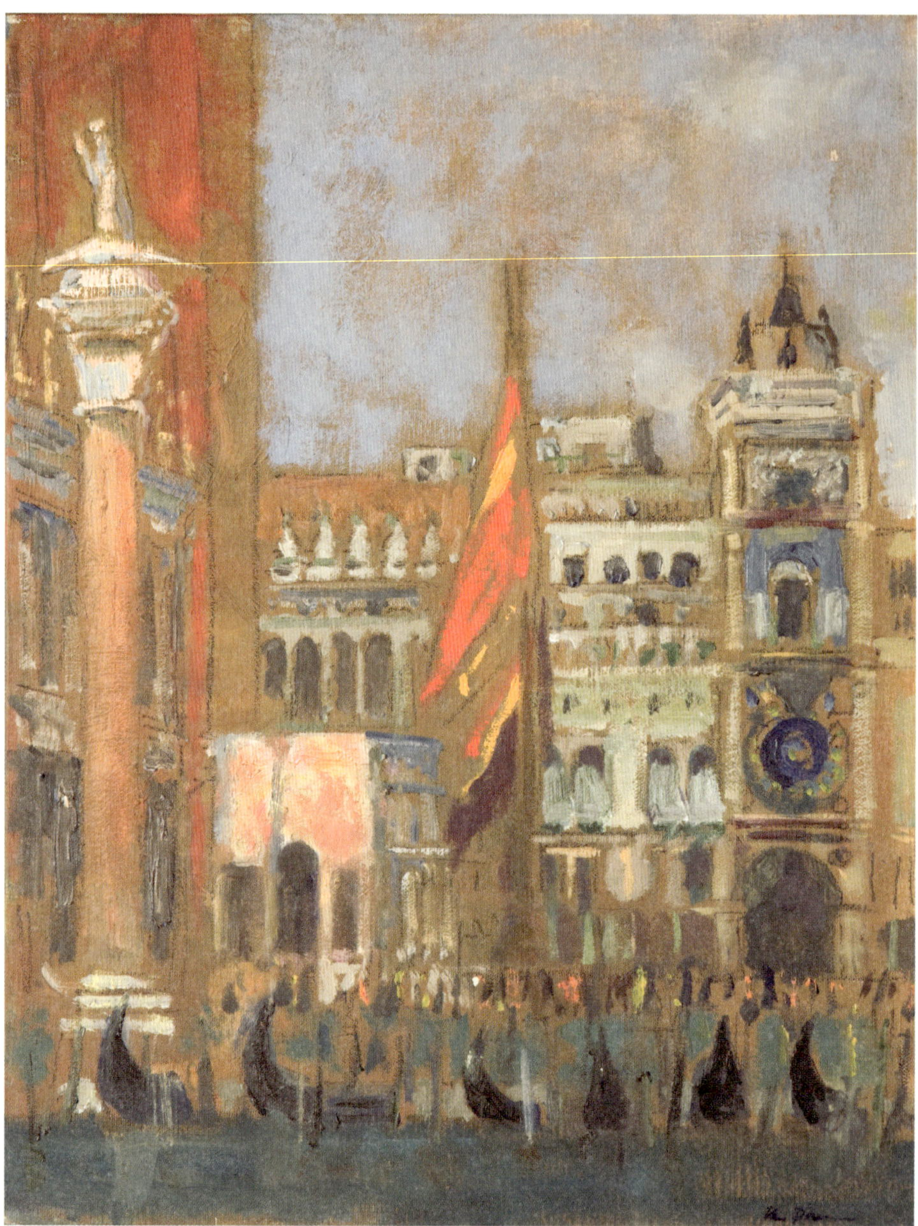

Flags in San Marco, *2008*

PREFACE

Theodore K. Rabb

Most people can remember how it felt when they first saw Venice. It's not quite like the "where were you when . . ." moment, associated in every generation with traumatic events, such as those of 9/11. This one is not only more pleasurable, but also evokes many senses rather than a solitary stab of memory. And it tends to be followed by a stream of images and recollections, resolving finally into an overall impression that each one of us can sum up as "our" Venice.

This book tells us about one such Venice – Adam Van Doren's – which crystallizes through the eyes and hands of an artist. It is not a common Venice, and in fact its precedents can be found only in the past three hundred years, even though the city itself can trace its origins back to the fifth century. For the notion that Venice's buildings and urban spaces are worthy subjects in and of themselves is a relatively new idea. We can see them in the background of famous paintings, such as Gentile Bellini's *Corpus Christi Procession in Piazza San Marco,* but they only became a focus of artistic interest in the years around 1700.

Why that happened we are not entirely sure, but in the late seventeenth century pioneers like Carlevaris and Vanvitelli began to find a market for "vedute," or views, of the city, and in the following century, in the work of Canaletto, Bellotto, and Guardi, these subjects became enormously popular. They appealed especially to tourists, who had been flocking to Venice since the Middle Ages, and who wanted to return home with colorful souvenirs of their visits. Eventually, though, the challenge of capturing the shimmering city on paper or canvas became the preoccupation of a galaxy of foreign artists as well as natives. Some of them, such as Turner and Sargent, are among Van Doren's heroes, and he makes sure we realize how aware he is of the footsteps in which he is treading.

That he has a few favorites is inevitable, and there will probably not be many who demur from his choices: the Ca' d'Oro, the Piazza San Marco and the structures that surround it, the major Palladian designs, and Santa Maria della Salute. Among the non-"vedute" painters, he is particularly drawn to Tiepolo. This may be a short list, but it is formidable, especially when one realizes that the buildings and canvases he identifies represent a tiny fraction of the countless masterpieces of art and architecture produced in a place whose population was probably never larger than 150,000. When faced by such riches, all one can do is sample.

What is amazing is how regularly one's own "Venice" overlaps with those of other people. I might put the Carpaccios in the Scuola degli Schiavoni nearer the top of my list, or the tombs of the early doges in San Zaccaria; but I wouldn't argue over the architecture, nor press the case that the altarpiece in San Alvise is Tiepolo's finest painting. Even more noteworthy are the small coincidences. When my wife and I first visited Venice, we stayed in the Calcina, as did Van Doren – and as did one of his inspirations, John Ruskin, more than a century before. It also happened that we got to know Regina Resnik and Arbit Blatas, and visited them on the Giudecca. Indeed, I spoke at a gathering in memory of Arbit in New York shortly after he died. Most remarkable, however, is the way that Van Doren's memoir conjures up – as only an artist can – the very feel and mood of a city that, in his evocation, seems so familiar that it is almost a part of one's family.

In his fourth chapter, for example, he writes of the beauty of

Venice at night. For Mark Twain, too, there was a special magic when darkness fell. As he described it in *The Innocents Abroad,* under the harsh sunlight the city appeared crumbling and decayed. He even compared it to a small Arkansas town. But then came the revelation:

> I began to feel that the old Venice of song and story had departed forever. But I was too hasty. In a few minutes we swept gracefully out into the Grand Canal, and under the mellow moonlight the Venice of poetry and romance stood revealed. . . . In the glare of day, there is little poetry about Venice, but under the charitable moon her stained palaces are white again, their battered sculptures are hidden in shadows, and the old city seems crowned once more with the grandeur that was hers five hundred years ago.

Twain's most popular lecture, in his tours across America, was "Venice by Moonlight" (he told his mother he felt "a few inches taller" because they went so well), and its fame may well have been one reason his countrymen began to flock to the city in the late nineteenth century.

Van Doren's chapter, entitled (in a nice operatic reference) "Queen of the Night," also suggests that this is a different city after dark. And he makes the case, as did Twain, through its music and its glinting lamps as much as through the specific reactions of a painter. In this case Whistler is the muse, but the effect is the same: to bring the image of a glowing scene of lights, water, and indistinct shapes vividly to mind.

For in the end it is because of the sensibilities of the painter that this book does so much to awaken our own thoughts about Venice. We may not share the peculiar problems of finding just the right spot from which to paint the Ca' d'Oro, or needing to stop and set up an easel in the Piazza San Marco just because the sun is hitting the Basilica from a revealing angle. But the emphasis on the play of light, on the unusual colors that fill the shadows, and on so many of the difficulties and delights that the artist encounters when trying to capture an evanescent scene – all these make one recall the breathtaking moments its visitors experience when Venice seems to become unearthly. My wife and I were once across the Grand Canal from the Salute on a morning so misty that we could not make out the church, less than 100 yards away. Over the next half hour though, the mist slowly evaporated, the sun began to beat down, and Longhena's enchanted building gradually grew and took shape in the mist. It is these moments of near-fantasy that define the city, and that Van Doren's art and prose summon up into consciousness.

What is also clear is how much an awareness of Venice's past, and of those who have traversed these waters before us, helps define our understanding of its beauties. Van Doren's book is full of tributes to those he treats essentially as his guides: not just artists like Sargent or writers like Ruskin, but also the family members and teachers who have shaped his engagement with the city. There is no doubt that, beyond the sheer exhilaration that is aroused by towers and domes rising out of the sea, surrounded by a constantly changing play of light upon the waters, it is the thought of all those who have been moved by these very sights that validates the wonder of the setting. If we enter the lagoon from the Adriatic, the scene that unfolds before us tells us forcefully how unique the delight of Venetians must always have been when they returned home. By reading these pages, and contemplating these pictures, we can follow Van Doren as he moves us yet again with the astonishment that is Venice.

FOREWORD

Simon Winchester

Adam Van Doren has a way with light. His painterly calling-card is, in its essence, illumination. It is opalescence, iridescence, brilliance. It is the subtly varied lights of dawn, of noontide, and of dusk. And as these paintings of the Venetian cityscape illustrate so vividly, it is the soft and languid interplay between warm Italian sunshine and the ancient stones and waters of this venerable city on its quiet lagoon.

And yet it is still more than that: for the artist manages to capture this uniquely Venetian phenomenon in a way that is perfectly, poignantly evocative. For me certainly, it conjured up in a madeleine-moment the very first time that I experienced the marvel that is the pure Venice light.

It was thirty years ago, late in a June afternoon of sultry heat, and as the train from Milan squealed across the industrial marshes south of Treviso I remember feeling pessimistically apprehensive about my first journey to Venice.

The auguries were less than perfect. I had flown to Italy from Hong Kong only the night before and was tired, crumpled. I was lugging with me a cache of heavy boxes of papers that I had promised to deliver to someone at the Biennale (this being an odd-numbered year), and the great festival was just about to begin.

I had very nearly missed the train. Smoothly polished and impossibly beautiful men and women in pastel linens – art dealers, I said to myself with a snarl – seemed to occupy all of the first class seats; in second class, a crush of Balkan tourists obliged me to stand all the way. My weariness must have dulled the visions of Verona and Padua as we passed them by, for I gazed out dully at their ancient skylines, unimpressible. I was nervous, too: all I had by way of introduction in the city ahead were two small pieces of paper. One bore a name and an address, untidy and mostly illegible, and, in brackets, the words "near the Ca' Rezzonico."

But then, in what seemed no more than an instant, everything became transcendentally different. The train slid effortlessly into Santa Lucia station, an eager porter took my boxes, and I followed him past the ticket offices and the peddlers and down the steps onto the small square. A square edged with water and lined with docks, with boats. I was put promptly into one of them, a water taxi – all varnished wood and the look of mighty expense – and once I handed the slip of paper to the driver, so he swept me away, deep into the thickets of the Dorsoduro. I confess I was briefly alarmed, ducked as we passed under low bridges, felt a need to shrink as we whizzed down a skein of tiny canals – Tolentini, Gafaro, Rio Novo are the names I recall – that zig-zagged, sunless, between ancient, red-washed buildings that were more precariously decayed, tide-marked, and beautiful than I had ever imagined.

After fifteen minutes or so the driver then slowed his motor, stopped beside a bridge, tied on to a stanchion, and helped me up with the boxes. What seemed like a solid brick of lira changed hands. He then pointed me down a mysterious-looking street, and told me, approximately, what to look for: a tall carmine-varnished door with a bell, to be found down an alley off an alley. It took me an age to find it, shifting my boxes along the street, kicking cats out of the way, wondering briefly what all the Venice fuss was about. This was still not quite La Serenissima I had supposed: it seemed more like a back street in Liverpool, or around the tenements of Fulton Street in the old days, only hotter.

But I duly found the door, and pressed the brass button, hearing the sound of ringing from deep within. There was eventually a shuffling and a scuffling, and an ancient man first cracked open the barrier and then revealed his face, smiling broadly and toothlessly as he did so. He was dressed in black and had the weathered face of a cobbler. He gathered me and my boxes into the room – a room that, surprisingly, had a floor that sloped down right into water and that ended in a doorway made of slats through which the sunlight shone and shimmered.

At the room's upper end, beside the doorway at which Alberto had welcomed me, all was dry, and there was a footway leading to a staircase and up into the house itself. But mostly this was the water-entrance to the house, and so there was a small dingy bobbing in the shallow water inside the room, and which bumped on the half-submerged flagstones. As the tide rose, so the canal water slopped lustily further and further into the bowels of the house, a translucent green and ever-spreading carpet.

Alberto could see I was fascinated. He was a little lame, yet he limped with grave dignity along the side wall and then with a flourish drew back the slatted gates. Afternoon sunlight then flooded in, the ceiling suddenly glittered with the reflection of a thousand golden dapples. He beckoned to me to look, to drink it all in.

It was beyond belief. Before me was the Grand Canal itself, no less, the madcap busyness of its great sinuous waterway spread out like some vast tableau, a private theatrical performance laid on just for me. There to the right was the immense, three-tiered Rezzonico mansion, no more than a few hundred yards away; the Accademia bridge was a little further down, and if I strained hard and leaned out over the water I could see the Rialto, too, a few hundred yards to the left.

There was a strange insistence about these cool waters, lapping as they did right into the heart of the very house where I was staying. You must venture out, they seemed to say. There was a small landing stage, and by chance a gondola was tying up to the striped pole at one end, and by even greater chance there came a sudden cry of welcome from within it – a friend of mine who lay on a cushion near the prow was waving to me, frantically. It wasn't a total coincidence. She knew where I would be staying and had come to meet me, to take me for an evening drink.

I mentioned earlier that I had two pieces of paper with me. The first was the one I had given to the taxi, and which led me to this exquisite miniature palazzo where I was now staying. The second, which I dug from my shirt pocket, was an introduction written from a mutual friend in London – a please be kind to this man letter, written to Arrigo Cipriani, the man who at the time ran no less a watering hole than – of course – Harry's Bar.

And this, without the slightest protest from my lady-in-the-gondola, was then where we promptly went. And which is why, as the sun went down on that first Venice evening, there we were: two old friends, sitting beside the tiny tinted windows of the bar, gazing out in a quiet rapture and sipping as we did so, and inevitably, pair after pair of fresh-made Bellinis. We were captivated: by the old palaces and warehouses of Giudecca out on the blue horizon, by the enormous white marble dome of the Basilica Salute just across the canal from us, by all the rest of the irresistible magic of Venice, which was laid out glowing and drowning in that evening's warmth, on every side.

Serene, eternal, perfect. Venice was at that moment for us what it has become for most who are fortunate enough to be able to stay there for a while, who are lucky enough to be able to drink it all in. Venice, the perfect stage set for an ever-unfolding dream, a place that after that inauspicious moment on the Milan Express became as I had long imagined – place of treasure, of secrets, and the embalming comforts of memory.

And a place whose tincture is all captured, so perfectly, in the lush score of the pages of Van Doren's Venice that follow.

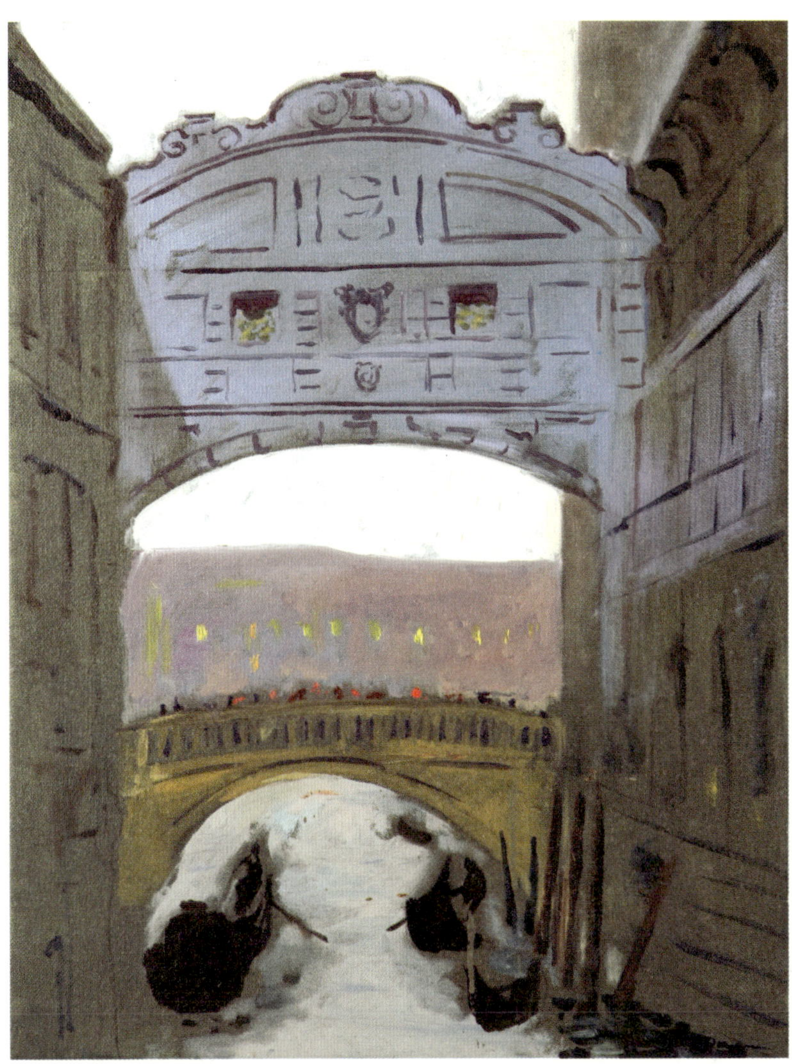

The Bridge of Sighs, *2008*

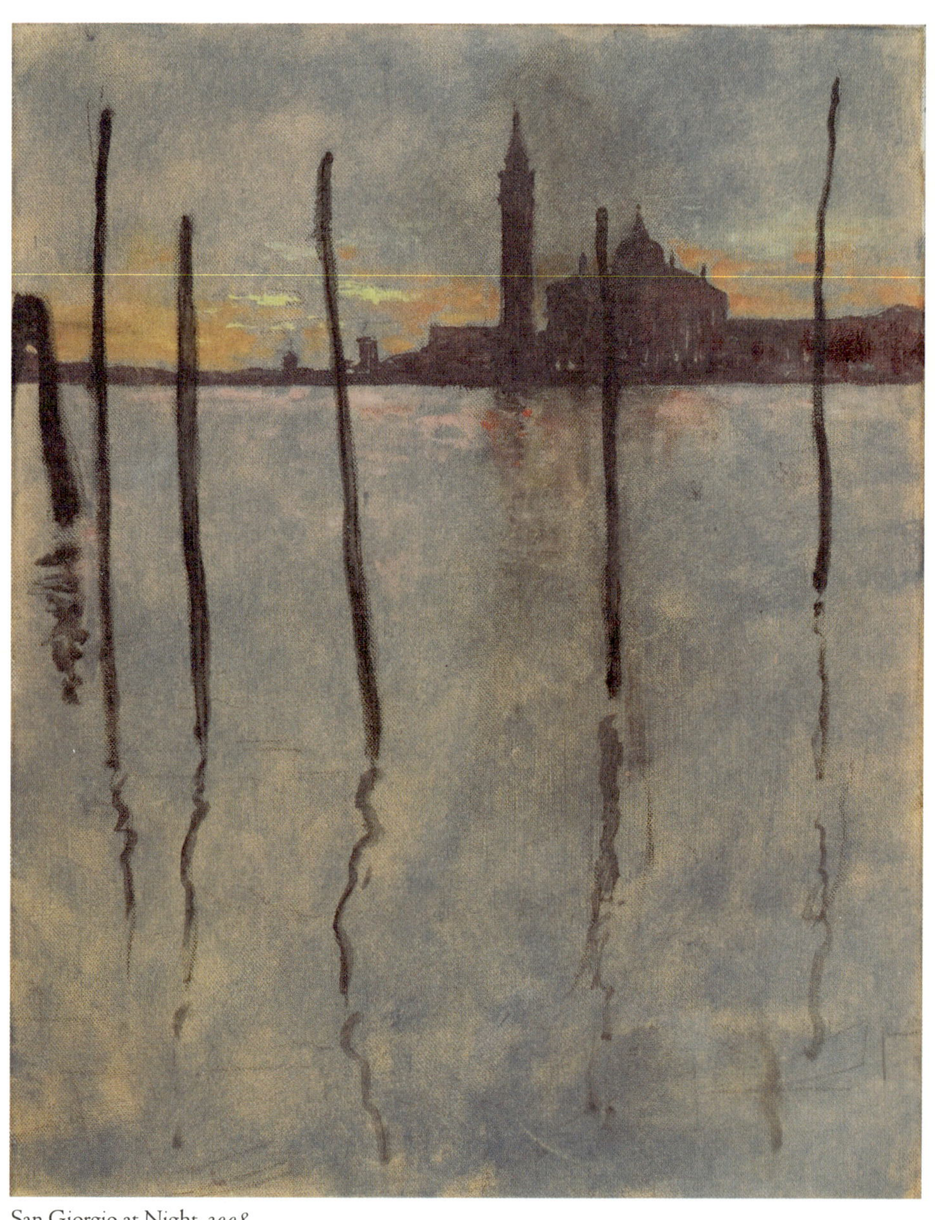

San Giorgio at Night, *2008*

"Venice still lingered on my mind when I arrived at the design studio . . ."

A WORLD AWAY

If you read a lot, nothing is as great as you've imagined. Venice is – Venice is better.

– Fran Lebowitz[1]

The winter of 1986 was barren and cheerless. Gray clouds scudded overhead, overshadowing the Columbia University campus like squat, menacing gulls. Students were holed up in dorms, huddled next to radiators. Finals loomed. Claustrophobia pressed in. I was trapped.

That December, wandering the depths of the architecture school, numb from a recent all-night charette study session, I noticed a brochure in the library announcing a summer program in Venice. The seductive cover showed a glossy photograph of the Salute church on the Grand Canal. *All inquiries to be made to Prof. Luigi Butera. References necessary.* I read the fine print. *Applicants to be selected based on an aptitude for drawing. Space is limited.* Despite the prerequisites, I thought my chances were good. Drawing was something I'd done for years, and Venice was a city I knew well. I jotted down the number for Professor Butera – suddenly the most significant person in my life – and determined that a summer abroad would be the perfect escape. But before I could seriously contemplate absconding to Europe, I had to satisfy my more immediate coursework: I needed to pass my semester review, which was only hours away.

Venice still lingered on my mind when I arrived at the design studio after lunch. Most of my fellow students were already there. They looked catatonic; some hadn't slept in days. The professors were silent as I nervously pinned up my elevations, rendered in pencil and watercolor. They deliberated for what seemed an eternity. When they finally spoke, I heard the words "painterly" and "inspired" – no faint praise from an architecture jury. That afternoon I scrounged around for Professor Butera's address and submitted my application. The sky seemed suddenly brighter, and I could breathe again. Elated and relieved, I was already sipping espresso in Piazza San Marco.

Lying awake in my dorm that evening, I pondered the possibilities. I thought of the expatriates who once lived there – Whistler, Stravinsky, Pound, Sargent, Browning, James, Byron, Brodsky – cultural luminaries in music, literature, and painting. The list was long. I felt presumptuous comparing my unfledged aptitudes to theirs. Unable to fall asleep, I got out of bed and stared out my window. I envisioned for a moment that the quadrangle below, outside Butler Library, was Piazza San Marco, and wondered if Venice would lead to anything significant – or if I was just being self-indulgent. Shouldn't I be looking for a *job*? My drawings for that day's presentation still lay sprawled on the floor. I looked at them again closely. In truth, I derived my greatest satisfaction from their use of watercolor – greater than any actual architectural problem I'd solved. I cared less about the requisite number of emergency exits and more about the quality of my rendering: the choice of colors, the shade and shadow. My years of art classes seemed finally to have paid off. Starting to droop, I closed my eyes and turned in.

Six months later I landed at Venice's Marco Polo airport, accepted

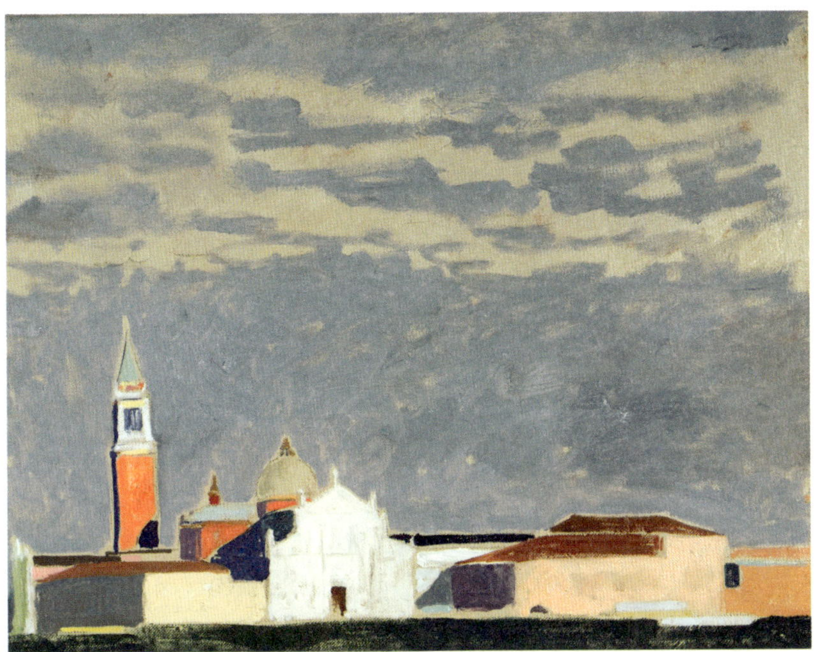

San Giorgio, *2009*

into the program. Boarding the *vaporetto* for my hotel, I started to plan my itinerary: the Palazzo Ca' Dario, with its colorful Renaissance façade; the Frari Church, which has a famous painting by Titian; and Campo Giovanni e Paolo, known for its equestrian statue of Bartolomeo Colleoni. My fingers itched; I couldn't wait to start sketching. But where to begin? It hardly mattered. In time, it would all make sense: I had decided to become a painter, not an architect – and Venice was responsible.

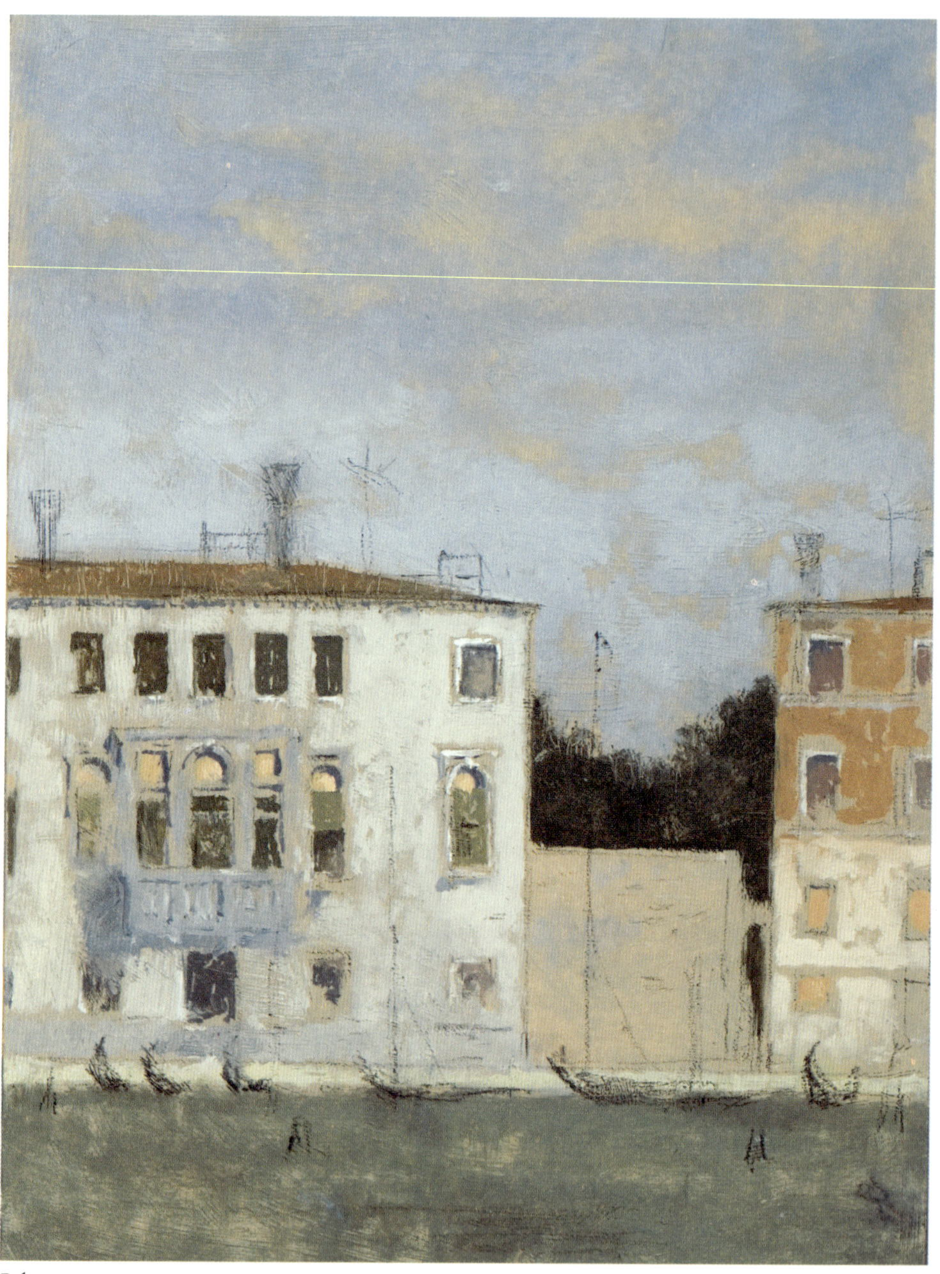

Palazzi, *2009*

"Like an unfurled Chinese scroll, the façades stretch end-to-end."

HEAVENLY MANSIONS

Its temples and its palaces did seem
like fabrics of enchantment
piled to heaven.

– Percy Bysshe Shelley[2]

I don't know what civilization is," the eminent art historian Sir Kenneth Clark famously remarked, while looking at the Cathedral of Notre Dame in Paris, "but I *do* know that I am standing in front of it."[3] The same could be said of the Ca' d'Oro in Venice, and there is no mystery why. It is a great building, not merely an excellent example of High Gothic – it would be beautiful in any style – but also because its proportions are perfect. Once the home of the Contarini family that supplied Venice with eight doges, the palazzo is not as big as some of its neighbors on the Grand Canal, but it doesn't need to be. Its façade, a hybrid of Moorish and Byzantine detailing, absolves it. Even its asymmetry beguiles.

I've painted the Ca' d'Oro, or House of Gold, both in oil and watercolor, but I'd be happy just drawing it in pencil. John Ruskin's *The Casa d'Oro*, rendered in 1845, is an inspiration. Though better known as an art critic, Ruskin was indeed a superb watercolorist in the finest British tradition, and this work, done on toned paper with gouache highlights, is a master class in technique. To some it looks unfinished – Ruskin left many areas untouched – but to my eyes it intimates just the opposite. Less is more, and he allows the viewer to fill in the rest.

I wondered where Ruskin sat when he painted this unique work. Judging from its perspective, it may have been done from a boat, facing the palazzo. Turner, the Romantic landscapist known as the "painter of light," hired gondolas to get the angle he wanted. Though tempted, I avoided availing myself of such expedients – and got lucky instead. Late one afternoon, walking near the Rialto, Venice's most famous bridge, I detected a narrow causeway directly across the canal from the Ca' d'Oro. There, in the sun, regal, ageless, and just like a postcard, I saw the greatest house in Venice.

I started to sketch rapidly, first drawing the second floor of the palazzo, with its intricately carved balcony and french doors; then adding the delicate finials at the top course. I carefully rendered the fenestration, which looked like tapestry. I used blues for the shade and avoided browns, which might muddy it. I applied one layer of wash for the background, then two. As daylight waned, the race was on. If I faltered now I had no one to blame but myself.

I laid my pad on the ground, stood back, and critiqued my sketch. Reasonably satisfied, I resumed working. Then a *vaporetto*, the ubiquitous small ferryboat peculiar to Venice, rolled in, heaving its rusty bulk into the dock like a wounded whale. The noise was jarring, an accepted abrasion in a city where waterbuses are the means of public transport. I had no choice but to wait for it to depart. When it finally did, the motor sprayed water all over my picture. My colors started to bleed together: ultramarine, alizarin, and yellow ocher were suddenly one. Miraculously, the picture was improved. *Only in Venice!*

Nearby, the fish merchants at the Pescheria were oblivious to my creative endeavor. Instead they were busy buying and selling the latest catch in the city's oldest open-air market. Squid, sardines, skate, sole, and crab lay heaped on long tables under an arched loggia. I took a break to watch them work. The merchants' sunburnt arms strained to lift the heavy crates; suddenly my backpack felt weightless in comparison. "Scusi!" one fisherman bellowed, as he pushed me aside with an armload of fresh *seppioline.* I quickly stepped back, and watched the frenetic activity from a safe distance. Then, as if a director had yelled "Cut!," the hour struck noon and everyone disappeared – mysteriously vanishing like in *The Cat in the Hat*. Empty cartons and crumpled wax paper lay strewn in piles on the worn stone pavement. The place was empty, ready to begin anew the next day.

Where had everyone gone? Italians in general, and Venetians in particular, savor their *siesta*, the long afternoon repast they enjoy until as late as four o'clock. Laborers, lawyers, doctors, shopkeepers – even artists – rush back to their families and enjoy homemade dishes, freshly prepared from the daily market, of prosciutto and melon, mozzarella and tomato, breaded veal – and of course *vino*. In the summer, the men take off their jackets, and women remove their high heels. They sit leisurely outside on wooden chairs, and eat and eat and eat. Sufficiently gorged, they refrain from dessert (sweets are less of an obsession than in America) and take a long nap instead. Nothing short of an earthquake will change this ritual. It is as sacred as the altar. Later, when the meal is done, kisses are heartily exchanged on both cheeks and the Venetians stagger back to work – a little tipsy, but restored. Not a bad life, I thought. I could learn something from this. My ambition, to produce as many paintings as possible in the shortest amount of time, sometimes prevents me from truly *seeing* the city – its atmosphere, its people, its *life* – which is as inspirational as the architecture itself.

Taking this cue, I created my own improvised *siesta*, found a comfortable corner between two buildings, and sat on a triangular stone bench built into the wall. These benches exist throughout the city, a gesture by Renaissance architects to provide citizens with a place to rest tired feet. Usually a tiny statue of the Virgin Mary is perched above, suggesting this act of charity had divine precedent. The seat was small, but it was just enough to relish my panini with peppered ham and Bel Paese cheese, smothered in olive oil. A bottle of refreshing Limonata, a sparkling lemonade, topped it off.

After digesting my meal, I wandered nearby to San Giacomo di Rialto, reputed to be the oldest church in Venice. It was built in 1287 for the ancestors of these same fishermen, and its pink stucco façade had three bells at the top, like a Spanish mission. Upon my entering the building and settling in one of the pews, the noise from the street abruptly ceased. The chaos outside was miraculously converted into cool, dim, and soundproof serenity. A cleric closed the heavy metal doors of the entrance and a muted thud echoed throughout the chamber. Variegated light passed through the half-moon window near the nave. I felt as if I had stumbled into the closet in C. S. Lewis's fantasy *The Lion, the Witch and the Wardrobe.* Looking around the church, first at the Renaissance paintings, then at the marble pediments, I was enveloped by one of those discoveries I've since come to expect in the dense, history-laden city of Venice. And though London, New York, Paris, and my hometown, Boston, have rich, eminently explorable architectural backdrops, Venice has one great transformative advantage: Mediterranean light. Startling at every turn, it surprises even the most jaded scholar.

Backtracking to the Ca' d'Oro, I surveyed it with fresh eyes. Its Gothic details are what give Venice its venerable cast. The city, after all, is medieval. Some of these details are specific to the Ca' d'Oro, but many, such as the pointed arches and fine tracery, are to be found in various incarnations throughout the city's six *sestieres*, or districts. A Darwinian evolution is at work here: those decorative motifs that survive have clearly stood the test of time. Ruskin, in his essay "The Nature of Gothic," organizes these differences into three grandiose categories: Servile Ornament, Constitutional Ornament, and Revolutionary Ornament – each with its own rarefied subtext.

Palazzo Ca'
Rezzonico, *1986*

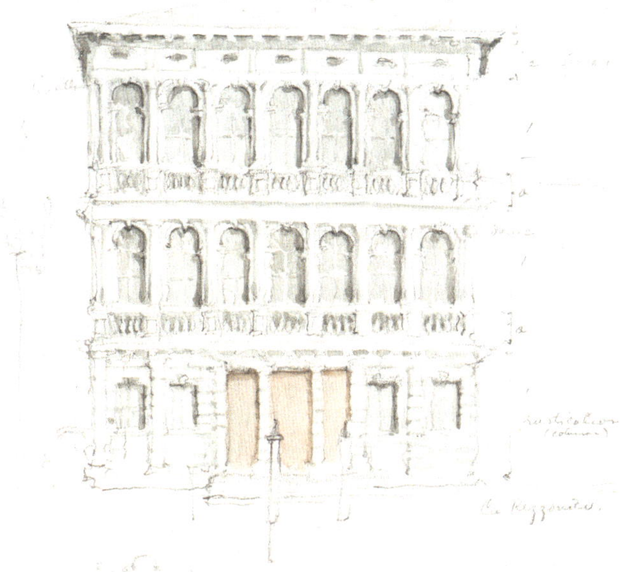

Ruskin was a social thinker – a fervent commentator on the economics and politics of his time – and he extended his principles to architecture. Favoring the Gothic style for its organic, human quality, Ruskin felt that "an architecture which is altogether monotonous is a dark or dead architecture; and those who love it, it may truly be said: they love darkness rather than light."[4]

But Venice, as much as Ruskin would have yearned for it, is not entirely Gothic. There are superb examples of Renaissance buildings, and the Grand Canal is a veritable museum for many of them. The easiest way to see these mansions is by boat. Like an unfurled Chinese scroll, the façades stretch end-to-end, following the canal's serpentine S curve in a continuous line. Baldassare Longhena, the seventeenth-century architectural genius behind the Salute, was responsible for two fine examples: Ca' Pesaro and Ca' Rezzonico, both of which were completed after his death.

Now and again a curiosity appears, like the Peggy Guggenheim Museum, once the Palazzo Venier dei Leoni. It has only one floor – the original owners never having completed the building – and was abandoned for centuries before Guggenheim bought it in 1958. Herself an eccentric, famous for oversize eyeglasses that prefigured Elton John, Guggenheim also had discerning taste in art. She thought the half-finished façade looked avant-garde and left it as is. The museum contains notable examples of cubist and expressionist paintings, one of the most celebrated works being the sculpture of a nude man by Marino Marini. He is seated on a horse with arms outstretched, his erect penis facing the Grand Canal. When I was a boy I found this intensely amusing, but the Venetians thought otherwise, and in deference to the Holy Father (or so I was told) they remove the offending appendage, which can be unscrewed, on Sundays.

Farther down the canal is a favorite palazzo of mine, Ca' Rezzonico. The home of Cole Porter during the 1930s, it has since become Venice's Museum of Decorative Arts. Clad in chalk-white Istrian stone, a sharp contrast to the weathered red brick structures nearby, the exterior is now discolored by smog. Whole sections blackened with soot form permanent shadows on the façade. (Even though Venice has no cars, the nearby industrial city of Mestre on the mainland, with its ominous smokestacks and refineries, is a constant threat to Venetian buildings – not to mention a blight on the horizon.) Fortunately, these toxic agents do not obscure the fluid lines of Rezzonico's façade. Divided into three equal stories, one neatly stacked above the other like a bridal cake, Longhena's structure forms a solid block on the Grand Canal. The arched windows on the first two stories run straight across the façade – a Renaissance version of the Bauhaus ribbon window – and they act to unify the front elevation. They are an excellent example of the classical architecture I'd studied in college, so much so, in fact, that I made Rezzonico the first building I drew in Venice. The palace was originally commissioned by the

Filippo Bon family, Venetian aristocrats who went bankrupt trying to finish it. Longhena died in 1682, before it was completed, but the Rezzonico family, who had made their fortune in the Turkish wars, bought the building and hired the architect Giorgio Massari to complete it according to Longhena's plans. Interestingly, a precise replica of the building, built by Stanford White in 1898 for Joseph Pulitzer, exists at 11 East Seventy-Third Street in New York.

I mused what it was like to go behind the walls of these Venetian mansions. There is rarely an opportunity to see their interiors unless you are one of the owners or are invited to a private party, and this usually requires ties to the Italian nobility, of which I have none. I settled for John Singer Sargent's excellent 1897 oil, *An Interior in Venice,* which is the next best thing to being there. Sargent, arguably America's greatest portraitist, was particularly skilled at rendering figures in a group setting. The painting depicts a distinguished family lounging in a living room at the Palazzo Barbaro, which Sargent often visited. In the background are tapestries, intricately carved Louis XVI furniture, large antique mirrors, crystal chandeliers, and elaborately decorated ceilings. All of the members of the fashionably dressed Curtis family – expatriates who were also Sargent's cousins – seem unaware of the outside viewer looking in, except for one: the formidable Mrs. Liddy Curtis. She stares out of the painting, composed and vigorous, with a hint of a restrained smile. Light from the outside window highlights her lace dress, while her husband is busy perusing a folio of pictures beside her. An attractive younger couple, standing behind them, exudes sophistication and class. Sargent captures this resplendent scene with rich, lustrous colors, and it is an astonishing group portrait. But apparently Mrs. Curtis felt otherwise: she rejected the painting because she thought it made her look too matronly. From her vanity sprang our good fortune. The picture was returned to Sargent and later found its way to the Isabella Stewart Gardner Museum in Boston, where it is now on permanent display.

Palazzo Grimani is another Renaissance building that enthralls. Built in the 1550s, it was designed by Sanmicheli, a student of Palladio. The structure resembles Rezzonico in its overall shape but is more muscular and robust. Now the Court of Appeals, Grimani features a triumphal arch at the first floor, a motif repeated in the floors above. It is one of the handsomest buildings in the city and, according to Ruskin, is "composed of three stories of the Corinthian Order, at once simple, delicate and sublime, but on such a colossal scale, that the three-storied palaces on its right and left only reach to the cornice which makes the level of its first floor."[5] Observing it by *vaporetto* once, I noticed the worn steps at the entrance, smoothed and polished by centuries of algae and seaweed. I tried to imagine noblemen from the sixteenth century arriving by gondola, daintily alighting in the high-heeled fashion of the day. It would have required the dexterity of Martha Graham to avoid slipping and falling. But such was the age. The aristocracy rarely, if ever, walked the narrow *calle* that surround these palazzi. Those passageways, redolent with garbage and worse, were the byways of the lower class and servants. Venice is more democratic now and its seamier side is accessible to all. Pigeons frequently used me as target practice in these back alleys, and I've had to clamber over cat ejectamenta in a mad game of Venetian hopscotch (Venetians seem annoyingly complacent about their pets), simply to get from one end of the street to the other. But given the eighteenth-century standard for hygiene, which must have been a sanitary nightmare, I can scarcely complain. Edward Gibbon, visiting in 1765, described the city as "stinking ditches dignified with the pompous denomination of canals." [6] Raw sewage was routinely flung into the streets, much to the chagrin of unsuspecting passersby, and the canals were a substitute septic tank, especially vulnerable during *acqua alta*, or flood tide. It is no wonder the aristocracy sought sanctuary in these palaces. The wealthy not only enjoyed the luxuries of fine art and architecture, they also literally held the higher ground above the teeming masses, remaining relatively free of the unpleasant realities of everyday life. There are good reasons why the second floor of a Venetian mansion is called the *piano nobile*, or "noble floor." And as Venice continues to sink – or the sea continues to rise, depending on which dire prediction you choose – this higher ground will be all the more fortuitous.

Not all of Venice's houses are palatial. Many are nondescript brick structures, held together (barely) by iron braces, with dilapidated balconies and peeling stucco, much like the slums of Naples; and sadly, too, rampant graffiti has taken its toll. Some of these buildings are five hundred years old. A few are older. Cannaregio and the ancient Jewish ghetto, districts where tourists rarely go, are where you will find many such structures. The nineteenth-century artist James Whistler, who loved the underbelly of Venice, was inspired by these picturesque neighborhoods and came to the city in 1879 to draw them. Working mainly with pastels, he returned to London the following year with well over a hundred finished works. When they were exhibited, the critics raved. It took Whistler's genius to elevate this unknown, often decrepit, side of Venice to the level of high art.

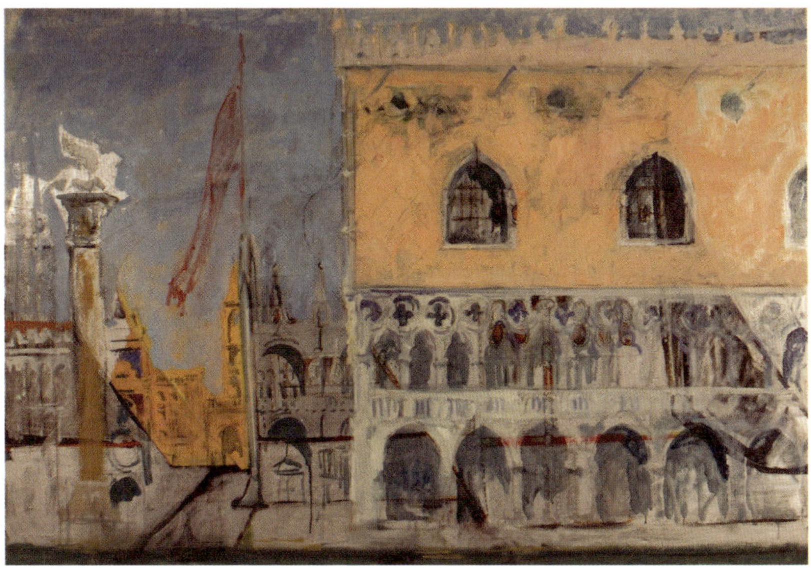

Gothic Fantasy, *2009*

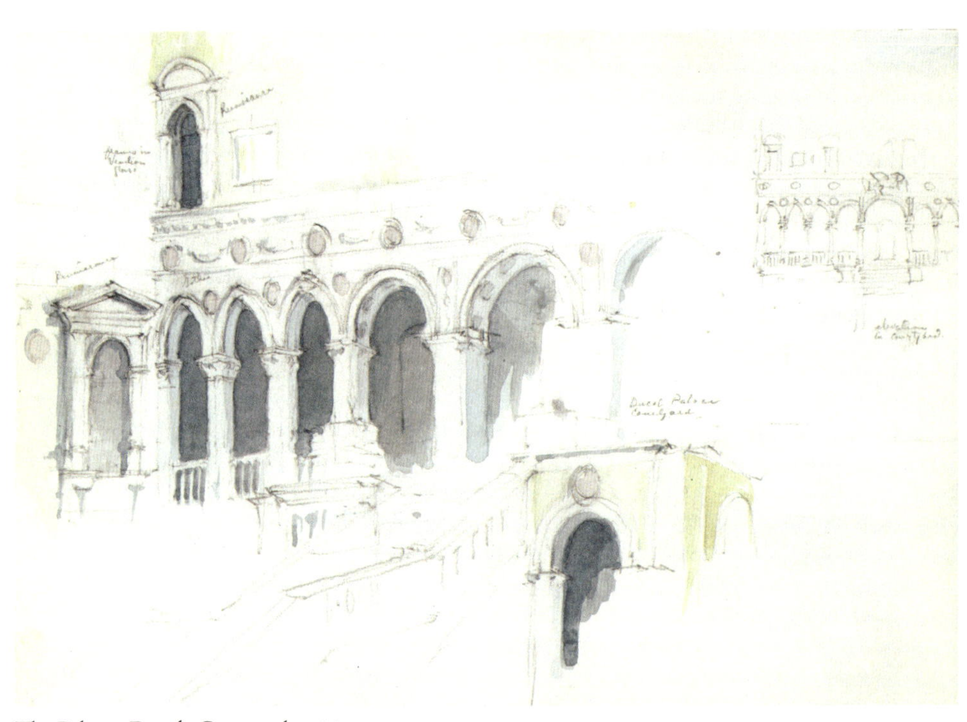

The Palazzo Ducale Courtyard, *1986*

"I employed a little traveling watercolor set, the kind Ruskin may well have used . . . crouched over a folding stool like an archaeologist mapping a pit."

CHANNELING RUSKIN

Thank God I am here! It is the paradise of Cities!

– John Ruskin [7]

Along the expansive Zattere, a promenade that is much wider than most of Venice's narrow streets, there is a stone plaque on La Pensione Calcina commemorating the art critic John Ruskin, who once lived there. Written in Italian, it gives the date of his residence as 1877. Few figures are more identified with Venice, or more controversial. His *Stones of Venice,* written in 1853, is a seminal work; opinionated and provocative, it is equal parts guide, polemic, education. Given that Ruskin was a Victorian, born at the start of Queen Victoria's reign, it is all the more striking – in an era known for its almost pathological restraint – that his treatise is so unabashedly exuberant.

I first came across *The Stones* in a reprint published in 1985, with an introduction by Jan Morris, the well-known travel writer. It includes reproductions of Ruskin's watercolors, which were omitted from earlier editions. Even a cursory reading of Ruskin's text reveals that he encompassed his subject like few before him, or since. But Ruskin was not merely not of his age; he was at heart a Romantic, linked more closely perhaps to the English poet John Keats than to his contemporary William Morris, the artist, writer, and early Socialist. Ruskin was famous, even infamous, for wandering Venice with a notebook and ruler, measuring cornices, columns, and mullions like a surveyor; and if he required a scaffold, he built one himself. The city became his obsession. His wife, in fact, considering him insane, wrote in a July 1879 letter to her mother: "Nothing interrupts him; and whether the square is crowded or empty, he is either seen with a black cloth over his head making daguerreotypes; or climbing about the capitals covered in dust, or else with cobwebs exactly as if he had just arrived from taking a voyage with the old woman on her broomstick."[8]

Fiercely determined to save Venice from itself, Ruskin abhorred the various "restorations" of the day, which he proclaimed were doing more harm than good. Venetians were woefully ignorant, Ruskin urgently insisted, of precisely what made their city beautiful. He tried in vain to discourage the city's efforts to restucco its façades, which he thought arrested the natural course of decay. Through his essays, photographs, and drawings, Ruskin launched a small crusade to document what he could before the city was renovated beyond recognition. "He came in haste after [Daniele] Manin's Revolution," wrote Morris, "concerned that all was lost."[9]

In the summer of 1986, during a summer spent abroad after college, I came to Venice without my parents for the first time. I was enrolled in a graduate program, affiliated with the University of Venice and Roger Williams College, to study the city's architecture. Like the other twenty students, I was required to keep a detailed sketchbook, form a thesis, and find my own digs, which I was fortunate to locate in the Calcina soon after I arrived. Off the beaten track, my small hotel was a short walk from the Accademia and the Salute; and from my window I saw the Giudecca, a strip of land a half-mile across the water, with glacier-like cruise liners gliding past. I walked across nearby Campo San Giorgio every day on my way to the *vaporetto*.

The tiny square was often empty, and it had a stone wellhead at its center. Built during the Byzantine period, this civic artifact was not only exquisitely beautiful and richly carved in stone, but it was also a remnant of a time when wells were integral to Venetian social life. I began to notice more and more of these throughout the city, and I recorded their salient differences in my notebooks. They were set low to the ground, and I often sketched them from a neighboring stoop.

At one time, my guidebook informed me, there were more than seven thousand wellheads in Venice; they provided fresh drinking water for its congested population and a locus to share daily gossip. I learned that underground cisterns were once used in each square to catch rainwater, through drains in the ground, which was subsequently stored within clay tanks. The cisterns were capped with wellheads, usually made of stone. As time passed, however, this ingenious hydraulic system grew obsolete, outmoded by more efficient, less picturesque engineering. Fascinated with these ancient relics, I made them the subject of my thesis.

Thinking of how to proceed with my project, Ruskin came to mind again, especially his meticulous drawings of architectural details. I bought a replica of a nineteenth-century sketchbook at a local art store. With a metal clasp on one side to keep it closed and a horizontal shape for drawing landscapes, it was small enough to slip into

Campanile, *1986*

my jacket, and I carried it around on my walks in Venice. In the margins, I made notes indicating my stops along the way – Campo Santa Margherita, the Giardini Pubblici, and Campo Morosini – adding dimensional lines and cross-sectional diagrams. Initially these thumbnail sketches were meant to be more analytic than artistic. But I was moved to create more compelling pictures, and, as I lavished on color and tone, the pages of my notebooks were soon emblazoned with a combination of images and writing, like vast illustrated letters.

After studying wellheads, I became immersed in another subject: bell towers. Likewise, they had their own mystique, indigenous to the city. Rising above the rooftops, their sonorous peals filled Venice day and night. Some lurched, seemingly ready to topple; others jutted straight upward, decorated with gargoyles or Serlian arches, a type of Renaissance window. Finding them useful landmarks when lost, I began to recognize them simply by their profiles. Campo San Barnaba and Campo Santo Stefano had exceptional examples, as did the Salute, which had two towers. "Naked and right like a mast of a ship," the French critic Hippolyte Taine wrote of these early skyscrapers, "the gigantic bell towers reach the sky and from a distance announce the old royalty of Venice to the travelers of the sea."[10] Inspired by these words, I climbed San Giorgio's tower once and beheld a panoramic view of the Adriatic worthy of a triptych. In the distance was the Campanile of San Marco, built in 1514, and almost one hundred meters high. Due to its poor foundation, it collapsed in 1902, but it was later rebuilt in a style as close to the original as possible: "Com'era, dov'era" – as it was, where it was – to quote Jan Morris.[11]

I developed a daily routine for my sketching. Each morning, with the sobriety of a Trappist monk, I set out at dawn to avoid the abundant tourists (loath to concede I was one of them), when the long spellbinding shadows of that early hour are especially striking. I took a tape measure with me, pacing out the width and breadth of the monuments. Depicting precise elevations and coloring them in,

I employed a little traveling watercolor set, the kind Ruskin may well have used, that had a miniature palette box, doubling as a cup for water (easily refilled in a canal), and a folding tray for mixing. People stopped and stared, and I indeed must have looked peculiar crouched over a folding stool like an archaeologist mapping a pit. Local children approached cautiously, taking breaks between pickup soccer games. "Bella! Bella!" one of them said of my picture, and it was the sincerest form of flattery I could imagine.

The best places to draw in the city were the large squares, or *campi*, so full of sun and air. They allowed me to get far enough back from the buildings, without straining myself, to see their details. These squares are "self-contained worlds," as the Venetian architect Sansovino wrote, "like the islands which were the origins of Venice itself."[12] Built over time, many have gained irregular, random-looking configurations, and there are nearly one hundred *campi* in Venice. Paved with gray-colored trachyte, a rough volcanic stone, they sometimes hosted bullfights in the nineteenth century. Campo Santa Maria Formosa was one I visited often. By no means as popular as San Marco, it is still a favorite among Venetians; and Canaletto's 1735 painting *Campo Santa Maria Formosa* is one of the best views of the square. I compared his picture with the *campo* today: minus the eighteenth-century garb, virtually nothing had changed. I spent several days stalking it from different angles, examining the locals going about their business: carrying groceries, filing into church, rushing to the *vaporetto*. In one corner there was a keystone at the base of the bell tower with the grotesque, contorted face of a man who looked like he'd been tortured.

Because I was alone most of the day (the other students were scattered throughout the city, busy with their own assignments), Ruskin proved an inspiring, if somewhat spectral, companion to me, and I often tried to conceive how he might have drawn what I saw. But it was just as well to admire him from afar; he was, by all accounts, stubborn, irascible, and mostly disagreeable. I probably would have disliked him personally, but how I admired his passion and draftsmanship!

The son of a wine importer, John Ruskin was born in London in 1819 and educated at Oxford. His early essay "Poetry of Architecture" was serialized in London's *Architectural Magazine* under the pen name Kata Phusin (Greek for "according to Nature"). In 1837, he published *Modern Painters* under the pseudonym "An Oxford Graduate," and it was there that his great subject emerged: J. M. W. Turner. Ruskin championed Turner as the leading artist of his generation, praising his practice of working from nature. In 1849, Ruskin turned to architecture: *The Seven Lamps of Architecture* and *The Stones of Venice* were major multi-volume tomes that have since become classics. His opinions dictated aesthetic taste for a century or more. Authenticity was Ruskin's mantra, and he despised, for example, Augustus Pugin's Houses of Parliament, which he considered a bastardization of the Gothic style. To his mind, this profusely detailed building was inferior because it was not *of its time*: it was neither built by guild craftsmen nor constructed by their methods. To me, Ruskin's rigid criteria at times seem excessive. I admire, for instance, the pseudo-Gothic campus of the University of Chicago, near where I lived for a decade, even though it was built in 1919.

The way Hercule Poirot pursued clues, Ruskin probed architectural details. In addition to drawing, he used photography – by then in wide use – to record his impressions. Preferring his sketches, which have more personality, to his photographs, I refrained from using a camera as a tool for drawing, and stuck with my pencil. I lugged Ruskin's books and Norwich's *A History of Venice* in my backpack for inspiration, and added Lorenzetti's *Venice and Its Lagoon* – written in 1923, but eerily still accurate – all fifteen hundred pages. In time, I enthusiastically learned to decode the differences between the more florid Byzantine and stately Romanesque. Later I shifted to the Renaissance and baroque, fully aware that Ruskin would have recoiled; he considered these styles nothing if not immoral. While Sansovino, Longhena, and Palladio were merely names in Columbia textbooks before, now I could easily identify their works throughout Venice.

When I had completed a month's worth of drawings, I submitted them to my instructor, Luigi Butera. He was sufficiently impressed to include them in an exhibit at the University of Venice. When his program concluded, I elected to stay on and study independently with the esteemed professor. We agreed to meet for lunch twice a week, at Caffé Seguso near the Customs House, where he conducted a mini-seminar over pasta. Butera, a short, nimble man with a nervous disposition, introduced me to the work of a man he admired: Carlo Scarpa.

Scarpa, who died in 1978, was an architect and artist and a master of detail. He designed only a few projects in his career, but they are all worth studying. Butera showed me Scarpa's renovation of the Querini Stampalia Foundation, a library near Santa Maria Formosa that was one of the only examples of contemporary architecture permitted by the Venetian authorities (Frank Lloyd Wright's designs for a palazzo in 1959 were rejected). Scarpa had a painter's eye, and I was attracted to his renderings in colored pencil. Butera gave me a poster of one of them, and also took me on a field trip to Verona to see a bank building the architect had designed. Chasing after him through cobblestone streets, I tried to keep pace with his manic step. We passed the ruins of a Roman theater as my teacher gesticulated wildly, comparing Scarpa's architectural detailing to the Gothic works Ruskin admired. Scarpa, a craftsman at heart, had no tolerance for shoddy work; he once made a contractor rip up a terrazzo floor three times just to get it right. He also had a great respect for history. Change doesn't come easy to Venice, and Scarpa knew this. That's one of the reasons he adored the city. Unlike some architects, who feel the need to obliterate the past in order to create the future, Scarpa had a much more sensitive and less defiant approach. His style was clearly modern, but his work incorporated subtle historical references that make it both contextual and timeless.

Professor Butera was also eager to teach me about historic preservation and invited me to meet a friend of his, the architect Giorgio Bellavitis, who was then restoring several Venetian buildings. I was given private access to some of Bellavitis's projects, many of which were still underway. Their exposed frameworks revealed wood beams and columns dating from the eleventh century; they felt as hard as rock. Miraculously, I learned, wood construction in Venice could last as long as steel. It seemed to make no sense, but neither did the idea of foundations made of piles buried underwater.

When I parted with Butera for the last time, it was with considerable regret. I'd fulfilled the requirements of his course, but there was more I wanted to see and draw. The professor encouraged my artistic aspiration and wished me well. As a gift, he gave me a copy of an exhibition catalog of his father, Remigio, a noted painter of still lifes during the 1940s. I thanked him and saluted him, a little ritual he and I had developed during our time together. Deciding on a change of scenery, I went to England, with the vow to stay longer in Venice the next time. I thought of my uncle and aunt, Charlie and Gerry Van Doren, both writers, who had found a way to split the better part of twenty years between Connecticut and Tuscany.

Packing my sketchbooks and bulging portfolio, now stuffed with watercolors, I caught a water taxi to the airport. Soon bound for Heathrow, I spotted the lagoon, a minuscule speck below, as we flew over it. When I arrived in London I transferred to a train for Cambridge, a city I had always admired but had never visited. I found quarters in a house where Charles Darwin had once stayed, and shared my room with a classmate from Columbia, Daniel Schecter, who came up from Berlin where he had been traveling. At Cambridge, English Gothic was on full display. King's Chapel and Trinity College kept my pencil busy. Some of it was derivative of the Gothic architecture I had seen in Venice, but there was an added layer of sumptuousness – the benefit of two hundred more years of history – and I envied the tutors who worked behind these stone edifices, some dating from the reign of Henry VIII.

From Cambridge, I arranged day trips to Oxford, where I made a point of seeking out the John Ruskin School of Drawing. John Updike mentioned it in an essay I had read and my curiosity was piqued. "It was part of a gentleman's 'equipment' in Victorian England," Updike once said, "to know how to draw."[13] I wondered whether this academy named for Ruskin still existed.

It did. And arriving at its entrance, with intricate carved wood molding, I walked in and experienced considerable disappointment. Nothing the art students were doing resembled classical drawing. They were, instead, immersed in huge canvases of abstract painting, the kind of imagery that would have made Ruskin expire. I'm not sure why I was so surprised; this, after all, was the twentieth century. But perhaps because I'd been living in Venice for so long, I had expected to see teachers bent over plaster casts expounding on the traditional methods of rendering shade and shadow. I left the Oxford building quietly, avoiding any queries of the staff, to make my way back to Cambridge.

I am very fortunate to have discovered Ruskin at that time in my life. Although I had majored in architecture at college, I was still struggling in those years with a nagging ambivalence toward architecture as a career. It was certainly appealing as a course of study – its curriculum synthesized both fine arts and the humanities – but I secretly wanted to become a painter, however dubious the prospects. My chosen subject matter was buildings, and Ruskin managed to bridge the best of both worlds: he was an *artist of architecture.* I saw no reason now why I couldn't aspire to the same.

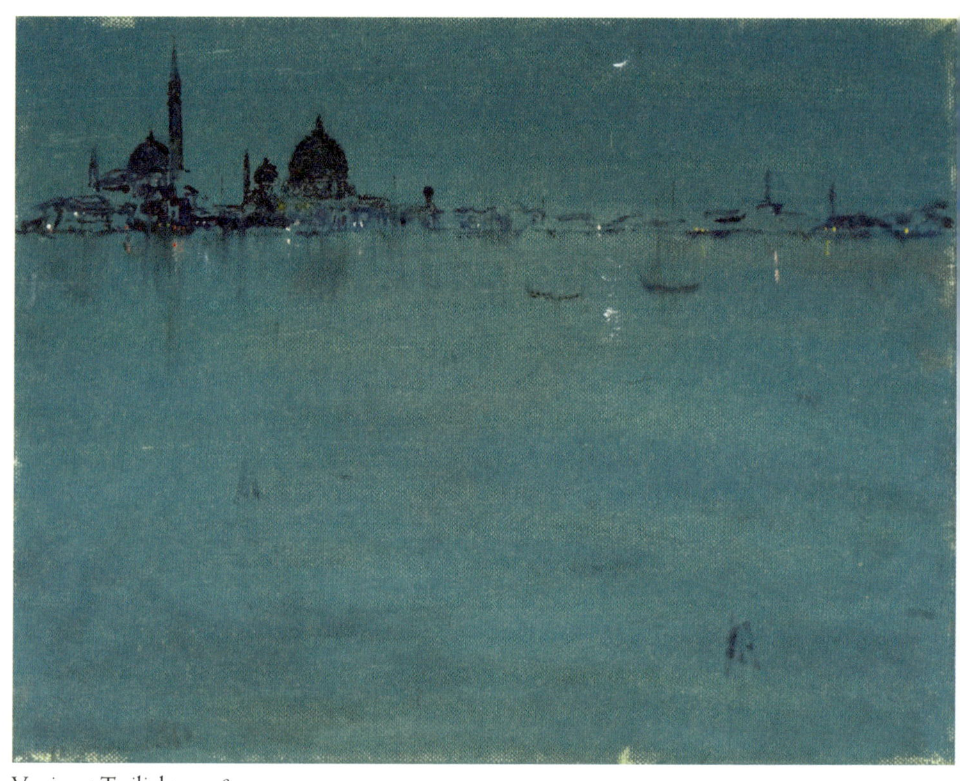

Venice at Twilight, *2008*

"Each city comes at a price, and for some the price of Venice might be its quiet. For me, it's a sanctuary."

QUEEN OF THE NIGHT

Do not apply too much water, the effect should be like breath on a pane of glass.
– James Abbott McNeill Whistler[14]

Night in Venice. It is not isolating or foreboding, like in some cities, nor is it somber. Soothing is how I experience it: more Mozart than Beethoven. Looking out from the Giudecca, one sees rows of street lamps stretching out in a long, low ribbon from the Zattere to the Riva Schiavoni, a walkway named for the ancient Slavs, or "schiavonis," who traded there. Familiar landmarks – the Campanile, Santa Maria della Salute, and the Palazzo Ducale – line the water's edge, lit up like dancers in a Degas painting. The skyline is Lilliputian compared to New York's – like one of those miniature cities in a bottle – but it resonates with jubilant architecture, even what's gone the way of Grey Gardens.

Aside from the occasional clanging buoy or carousing reveler, the city is remarkably quiet at night, especially when one stays clear of Piazza San Marco and the Rialto. Motorboats slow to a crawl, and even the discos keep the volume down. After all, many of the natives are fishermen and must rise early. (An exception to such civilities is the Carnival in February, its raucous evening a well-deserved reward to Venetians for being so quiet the other 364.) For me, such solitude is unusual; New Yorkers must endure a cacophony of car alarms, ambulances, the metallic thrum of traffic, and raucous midnight conversations that pierce their way through sleep at all hours. It is a necessary evil, perhaps, in exchange for living in the art capital of the world. Is it worth it? I suppose you can justify anything, but luckily in Venice I don't have to. Each city comes at a price, and for some the price of Venice might be its quiet. For me, it's a sanctuary, a place to reflect and wonder, like the seashore on Martha's Vineyard where I have spent many summers.

James Whistler captured this sweet serenity with perfect pitch. His series of paintings entitled *Nocturnes* have forever altered how we see Venice, in the way Piranesi, with his etchings of monumental ruins, forever altered how we see Rome. Beyond shades of gray and dots of yellow, Whistler's works, completed between 1866 and 1876, are little more than pure atmosphere, and pure genius. It is minimalism at its best and the artist knew as much. To John Ruskin, however, the leading critic of the day, these pictures could hardly be called art. To him, they were contemptible, even sacrilegious, precisely because the paintings took so little time to create. (Similar, I suppose, to judging a piece of music by how many notes it contains.) Whistler considered such superficial criteria ludicrous: what mattered was what the paintings *looked* like, not how they were *made*. Of course, he was right, but he had to file a notorious defamation case in 1892 to prove it, which became a sensation in the London papers. Cross-examined by lawyers, Whistler was asked, "How long did it take you to knock off that *Nocturne*? . . . Only a day? . . . Is that for which you ask 200 guineas!"[15] Ultimately, the judge ruled in favor of Whistler, agreeing that Ruskin had inflicted undue harm on his reputation, but the vindicated artist was awarded a mere farthing for his troubles, and was left with crippling debt. In the end, ironically, Ruskin's credibility suffered more than the accused. The combative critic had been egregiously blind to what was right in front of him – a modern painter not *of* his time, but decades *ahead* of it.

If the *Nocturnes* seem simple at first glance, they are also emphatically complex. Whistler invents light where there is none, using tone for effect, and creates perspective by deftly adjusting the height of the picture plane. His luminescence is abstract, even lyrical (you can practically hear Debussy in the background), and it influenced later artists such as the Americans George Inness and John Twachtman, Claude Monet, and the English artist Walter Sickert, among others. (However, Turner, to a large degree, was the precursor to them all: his night scenes of Venice are as modern as Rothko's visions, with their moody patterns of diffused, saturated light.)

My memories of nocturnal Venice are less romantic than Whistler's, perhaps, but they have their own picturesque moments. They derive from vacations with my parents and brother in the 1970s. We stayed at the Hotel Cipriani, a family tradition begun by my grandparents, Lydia and David, who first came there in the 1950s, shortly after it opened, and thereafter reserved the same room every August for twenty years. When David, a physician, died in 1972, Lydia went alone or accompanied us. In the early days the Cipriani was not as exorbitantly expensive as now, when a Fanta soft drink by the pool can send you to the poorhouse. My father, John, was an editor at Encyclopædia Britannica, and my mother, Mira, an enamelist – hardly the jet set – and they thought nothing of booking a prime suite overlooking the gardens. The Cipriani's one great extravagance was its pool – until recently, the only one in Venice – and it provided a seductive alternative to sightseeing on hot days.

The Cipriani also had a private launch that shuttled guests back and forth at all hours to San Marco. We often took a ride after dinner, and sitting at the back of the plush teak boat, with its glistening layers of polish, I would watch the churning water as we passed the lights of San Giorgio and the Giudecca. As we arrived at the Piazza, waiting attendants from the hotel escorted us onto the dock. As was our custom, we made a beeline for Florian, a café that has been an institution since the early 1800s, and, finding a table on the square, we would watch the band play its version of Italian elevator music. Sampling cannoli, tortoni, zabaglione, and biscotti, I once requested the schmaltzy song "Arrivederci Roma," a guilty pleasure even then. Agile waiters wiggled between tables like eels, and when the music stopped and the café started to close, we would linger till midnight, savoring the moment. Returning to the Cipriani by boat, I remember looking back at the lights of the Ducal Palace and wondering if I might someday return and paint what I'd seen. Years later, I did.

I have returned to Venice several times since, but never again to rooms at the Cipriani. In 1992 my wife Charlotte and I came to the city, shortly after we were married. We stayed at the Accademia Hotel, a small but reputable *pensione* in a private section of the Dorsoduro, the area across the canal from San Marco. We arrived from Nice, where I had joined her on a business trip, and on a whim we took an after-midnight tour of the city by gondola. We found a willing gondolier, and, after paying him the equivalent of our airfare, he steered us safely away from the busy Grand Canal. Maneuvering like a halfback, he ducked under low bridges, nearly decapitating himself. Intricate shadows formed cryptic patterns on the buildings, a collage of peeling stucco, chipped paint, rusty iron, and graffiti. We passed shuttered houses, hearing muffled voices and the sound of a television. Looking up through this narrow canyon of buildings, the sky was barely visible; illumination came mainly through the windows of those few homes where people were still awake. We reconnoitered where Mark Twain and Byron had stayed. A stray cat peered at us from an open window, his eyes following us like balls at a tennis match. Empty plastic bottles and candy wrappers floated by, and the canal began to stink. The romance fled. We pulled our arms to our bodies to avoid touching

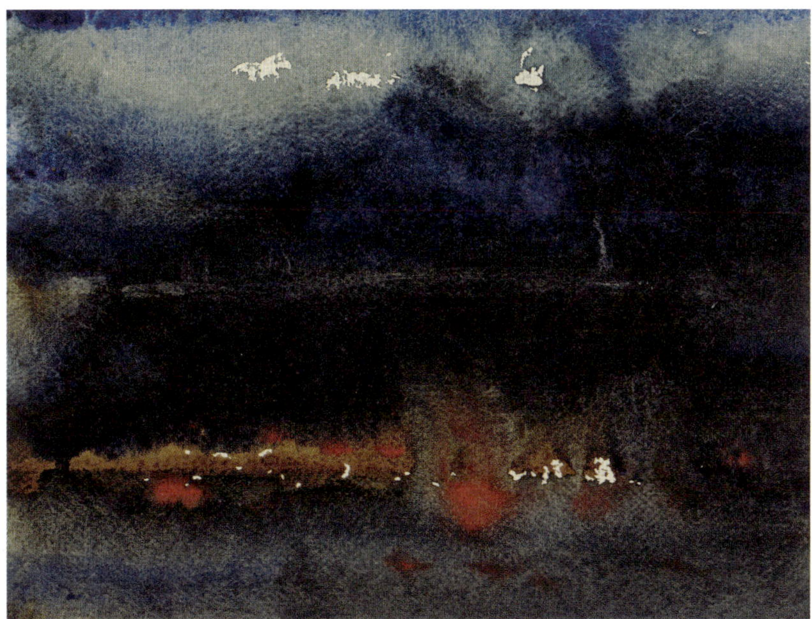

Night scene, Giudecca, *2010*

the water. The viscous surface made us queasy; we could imagine the rats swimming just under it. When our little adventure ended we were both secretly relieved.

After tipping the gondolier we started back to our *pensione*. We tried using maps – an exercise in futility – and revolved in circles instead. Venice can swallow you whole. Its streets are seductive: you can follow one path that looks promising, but soon find yourself at a dead end. Despite the situation, we didn't panic: Venice, though at times exasperating, is not dangerous. No one followed us, and we didn't care if we got lost. There was a perverse pleasure in discovering how grossly inadequate our sense of direction was, and when the Rialto, a familiar landmark, came into view, we felt triumphant, and headed home – shaken but ready, somehow, for more. Ironically, I had once prided myself on my ability to find the best shortcuts in Venice. I practiced doing so when I was living on the Dorsoduro and attending daily Italian classes at the Scuola Dante Alighieri, near the Arsenale, the former shipyards. I timed myself and once went out in the pitch darkness to see if I could do it. I may as well have been blindfolded, but managed to arrive in one piece.

The penultimate evening event in Venice, after Carnival, is the Festival of the Redentore. It takes place in the third week of July and is a great excuse for Venetians to party. Its origins are more sobering: a celebration to mark the end of a plague epidemic. Following tradition, a row of floating barges is linked together for the day, making a bridge over the Giudecca Canal and allowing Venetians to "walk on water" toward the Redentore. Fireworks boom well into the night, rattling the very foundations of the buildings. In 2003, when Charlotte and I returned to Venice, we witnessed this spectacle along with our twins, Abbott and Henry, then six. Abbott sat on my shoulders while the pounding noise reverberated across the city like thunderbolts. She was terrified. Her small hands clutched the back of my neck with the force and tenacity of a bench-presser. I looked up and tried to reassure her, but it was like trying to calm a Londoner during the Blitz. What had I been thinking? Abbott, at that age, couldn't even tolerate the modest Fourth of July celebrations we saw in Connecticut every summer. My fearless son, Henry, had the opposite response, racing through spectators' legs with glee as I did my best to keep up with him. When the fireworks ended, Abbott released her hold on my forehead. I pulled her down off my shoulders and hugged her. Her whole body exhaled at once. Out over the water, lights from boat masts strewn with flags tinged the lagoon. With the revelry stopped and the streets no longer vibrating, Venice returned once more to its serene and haunting self.

It takes a certain ingenuity to render night scenes like the Redentore festival, especially *in situ*. Once, I found myself painting the spectacle from the Giardini Pubblici, a section of Venice well beyond Piazza San Marco, near the Biennale exhibit. The sun had set, and a striking silhouette of the city appeared on the horizon. Domes and spires rose from the mist. Specks of light from boats in the harbor flickered in the distance. With no other illumination than a street lamp, I tried to work in the dim light. But on mixing my palette, I could barely see my colors (ask any woman who has tried to apply makeup by candlelight). Reds became greens and greens became browns. I took off my glasses and squinted, but could only see a thick haze, like a foggy windshield. How had Whistler managed under such adverse conditions? I thought of the American artist Guy Wiggins, who not only painted night scenes but snow scenes as well, which are even more challenging. How he had pulled it off without braving a blizzard is difficult to know; he either had great visual memory or worked from photographs. Atmospheric effects like the ones Wiggins created were highly sought after by collectors, and he made his name with them. Childe Hassam, the Gilded Age American Impressionist, whose studio in Manhattan I now occupy, prided himself on his ability to render, in addition to snow, rain. His puddly streetscapes, with hansom cabs set dramatically against the black sky, are some of his finest works. Unfortunately none of them has ever turned up in my studio, though I haven't stopped looking.

More and more I have trained myself to work from memory, which can be a pleasing alternative to painting *en plein air.* I've come to appreciate, or at least tolerate, the Venetian street artists who, despite their formulaic, repetitive approach, can whip out a canal scene straight from their heads. It is liberating and often gratifying not to be bound by only what's in front of you. As Robert Frost said of free verse: it is like playing tennis without a net. For that revelation, I have my mystical nights in Venice to thank.

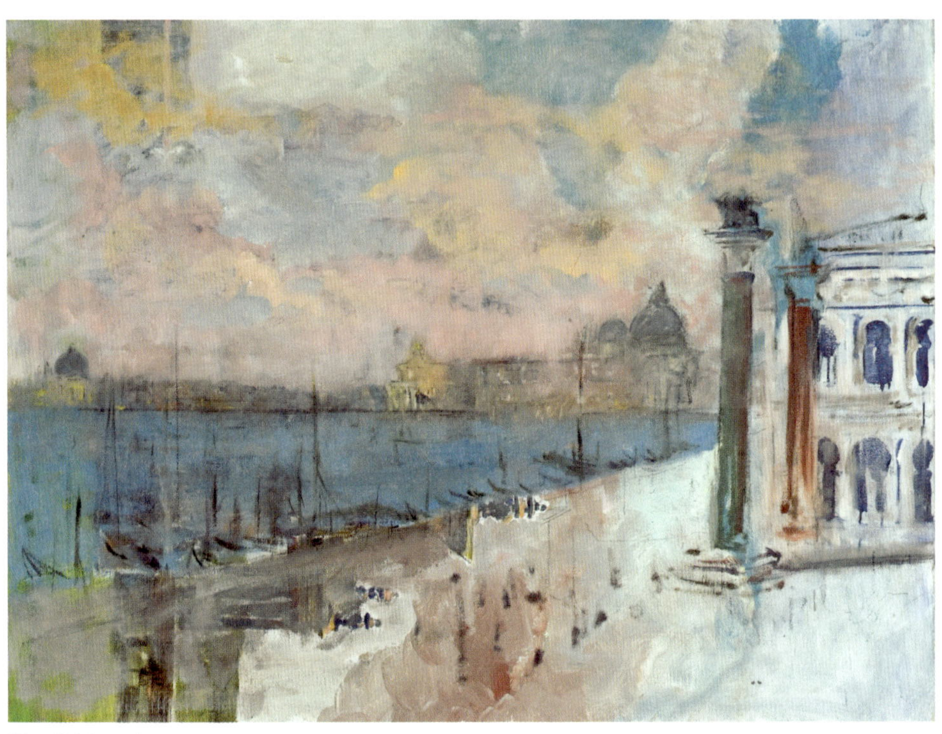

Riva Schiavoni, *2010*

"[Arbit] often asked me to draw outdoors with him. I was self-conscious . . . but I dared to join him once."

ARBIT AND REGINA

Regina and I did not know that we would make our lives together and that by chance we would find our Venetian home on this island [the Giudecca]. We have often repeated Carmen's words in Act III: "Le destin est le maître."

– Arbit Blatas [16]

At the far end of the Giudecca, near where the old Stucky Flour Mill used to be – it is now a four-star Hilton – there is a low three-story house with an attached art studio. For many years it was the summer residence of the artist Arbit Blatas and his wife, Regina Resnik, the former opera singer. Arbit died in 1999, but Regina still lives there. The two made a festive couple and had a flair for the dramatic. Neither of them was Italian – Arbit was from Lithuania and Regina from the Bronx – but they were never considered outsiders in Venice. On the contrary, they were always warmly embraced by its society. I remember them arriving one evening to attend an opening of Arbit's work, standing arm in arm in a gondola and gliding across the water as in a Fellini movie. Somehow they managed to keep their balance. When they pulled in, Arbit kissed Regina's hand, helped her up onto the dock, and bowed to the crowd like a matador.

Arbit was tall, flirtatious, and very funny, and his company provided the wattage to light up any room. Debonair even in his eighties, he wore a white suit and white fedora pitched at a rakish angle. He would arch one eyebrow and flip back his sunglasses like a movie star. But this was only an act; Arbit was a serious artist who worked harder than any I've ever known. A mixture of spontaneity and energy, he once painted a full-length mural of Regina in operatic costume in their dining room in Venice. She looked imposing, holding a long staff in front of her – just a touch of Veronese on the Giudecca. When Arbit wasn't painting, he was making sculpture, primarily of famous persons he knew, including Marcel Marceau and the Expressionist painter Chaim Soutine. Arbit loved people and sought their company often, and it's a mystery to me how he found time to produce as much as he did. Most of his work was done in his studio, which opened out onto the *fondamenta*, with majestic views of the Dorsoduro.

Regina, now in her eighties, is less gregarious but shares Arbit's sense of humor. She is fond of telling jokes and is knee-slappingly good at it. She has thick blond hair atop a strong face and speaks with authority and intelligence. For several years she has been teaching master classes at Mannes College, The New School for Music, and though she does not suffer fools gladly, her compliments can mean the beginning of a promising career. Regina was born in 1923 to a middle-class family and studied at Hunter College in New York, where she performed the male leads in Gilbert and Sullivan operettas. She was one of the youngest singers ever to debut at the Met, as Lenora in Verdi's *Il Trovatore*, and became a sensation overnight. Carmen, from the Bizet opera, was one of her signature roles, and she performed it, among others, all over the world, from London's Covent Garden to Milan's La Scala. At a recent benefit at Lincoln Center, I heard an archival radio broadcast of her singing at the age of fifteen. She already possessed the operatic voice of someone twice her age.

I first met Arbit and Regina as friends of my family. Among the varied legacies of my parents and grandparents are the lasting friendships I've made with the people they knew. My grandmother Lydia had known Arbit since childhood, ever since they first met in Riga, Latvia, sometime before the First World War. Arbit retained a fondness for her all his life and made her blush when he recalled moments of flirtation in their youth, recollections that embarrassed me when I was younger. They shared a common past in Eastern Europe, and despite living in America for many years, both had thick accents. Their banter would shift from English to Russian and back again, and though I'd studied Russian at Columbia, I could seldom make out what they were saying. After Arbit married Regina in 1975 – the two had met in 1971 when Regina was making a film version of *Carmen* in Hamburg – they often came to my grandmother's apartment in New York, especially on New Year's Eve.

In 1982, when Lydia joined my parents and me on a trip to Venice, Arbit and Regina were generous enough to find a place for us to rent for a month. They located an apartment belonging to their friend the Countess Maria Premuda, who lived in a gracious, though not overly grand, residence on the Zattere. Premuda shared it with her longtime maid, also named Maria, who not only cooked and cleaned but was a devoted companion. They traveled together like an old couple, visiting Trieste, a city on the Dalmatian coast, during August, when Premuda rented her home. When we stayed there, we felt like Venetian royalty; the living room had french doors that overlooked the water with views of Il Redentore, and light pouring in as in an Edward Hopper painting. The study had archaeological artifacts from Crete, Sardinia, and Sicily, which Premuda's late husband had collected during his years in the shipping business. The Greek vases, precariously perched on high shelves, were museum quality and it made me nervous just to look at them.

One three-day weekend that summer, my parents took a trip to Florence, leaving my brother Dan and me, both just past our teens, on our own. Premuda and Maria had not left yet for their holiday, and in the interim lived in an attic bedroom right above us. We dined with them each night, enjoying Maria's mushroom risotto, tortellini Bolognese, and *palacsinta*, a Yugoslavian dessert made of thin crêpes and fruit preserves. Both women made a great fuss over us, Premuda dishing out monikers like *cucciolo* and *bambino,* while Maria assiduously ironed our clothes every morning even when we didn't ask her to.

Then one day everything abruptly changed. That morning Dan and I bumped into an old friend, Julie Schillinger, near San Marco. We had all grown up together in Connecticut, and she now was backpacking through Europe with a girlfriend. We invited them to see our house, a far cry from the youth hostel they were staying at. After lunch, Maria came down as usual to prepare dinner - but spotting our guests she was horrified, and ran hysterically to alert Premuda. The countess was equally aghast and shrieked in mystifying swift Italian that we had brought *prostitute* into her house. Deeply religious Catholics, they both blanched, of course, to think we were attempting to live in sin. But once the relationships were explained as "school friends" and the confusion sorted out, Premuda apologized and pretended to accept the ways of young Americans. When I told Arbit and Regina, they were amused by the misconception, but not surprised at such a reaction from their generation of Venetian ladies.

In New York, Arbit and Regina's apartment had a living room that doubled as his atelier. The small one-bedroom residence, in a brick Midtown tenement, had a large skylight and was filled with Arbit's artwork. Paintings lined the walls, leaned against the fireplace, and overflowed on the chairs. In the foyer, posters of Regina's operas hung in rows up to the ceiling. The furniture consisted of an ample L-shaped couch, comfortably cushioned chairs, and a large circular coffee table. Regina had a small desk that she used for her correspondence. Despite the tight quarters, they entertained often. To them, artistic creation

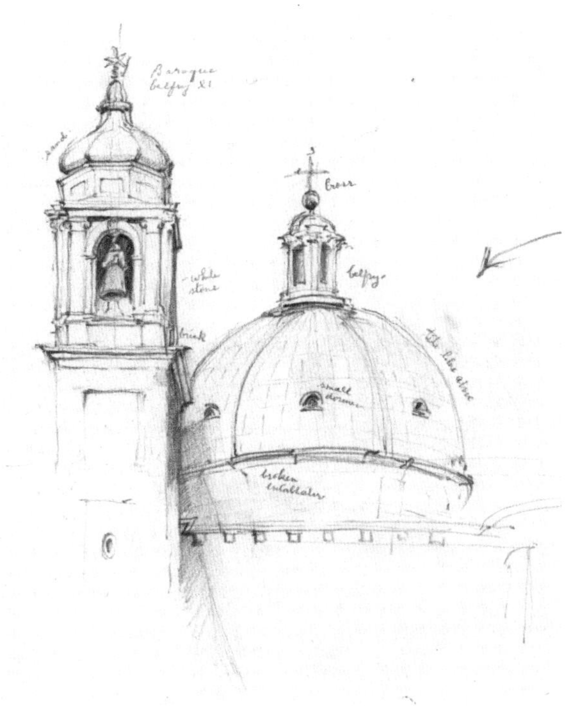

Bell tower, I Gesuati,
1987

and the joys of social life were interchangeable. When I visited them on occasion, Arbit liked to share with me what he was working on. He would beckon me to his easel to inspect his latest picture: "Did I get the sky right?" he'd ask. "Is the color too dark?" I was flattered that he responded to my critiques, and pleased when he touched up any area I had indicated. I was especially fond of Arbit's nightscapes of Venice. They were painted in deep blues and purples, with spots of yellow and orange. Scenes of the Festival of Il Redentore with fireworks blazing were among his most exquisite.

When I showed him my own work, Arbit was impressed by my sketches. They were very detailed, drawn with a precision I had learned in architecture school. Arbit's style was more impressionistic. He envied my training, while I envied his spontaneity. He often asked me to draw outdoors with him. I was self-conscious and unsure how to keep up with his ebullient personality, but I dared to join him once. We talked as we painted, and he confided to me how he had survived the Holocaust as a child from a Jewish family, fleeing to France where he studied painting. He became the youngest member of the famed School of Paris and had met Picasso, Soutine, the Cubist sculptor Jacques Lipchitz, and the French Fauvist Maurice de Vlaminck. He had sat with them in cafés on the Left Bank and had posed for them, as they did for him.

Arbit had a loyal following for his work, but none more admiring than Regina, his muse and confidante. She appreciated his talent and nurtured it, arranging exhibits and becoming his unofficial agent. She was savvy, tough, and practical; and since her own days as a diva were beginning to fade – she had by then retired from the Met – she was able to devote more time to assist him. But, like Arbit, Regina was an indefatigable worker. While she helped her husband, she also resiliently revived her career in the 1980s with roles on Broadway, first as Madame Armfeldt in *A Little Night Music* and then as Fräulein Schneider in a 1990 revival of *Cabaret*, for which she was nominated for a Tony Award. I remember seeing her in both of these productions and being awestruck by her superb artistic range.

Arbit's career thrived even in his advanced years, with numerous projects to keep him busy, including commissions, monographs, and appearances. In Venice, in the old Jewish ghetto, he completed a series of bas-reliefs of the Holocaust that won him considerable acclaim and are now on permanent display. (Regina, never short on talent, also made a documentary on this same ghetto for public television.) More portraits of prominent musicians, dancers, and artists followed: the conductor Leonard Bernstein, the choreographer Harold Prince, and the legendary cellist Mstislav Rostropovich among them. All the while Regina was a constant presence, and the two remained inseparable in their whirlwind life.

In 1991, as a wedding gift, Regina gave me a handsome limited-edition volume of Arbit's prints, which included portraits of Regina. The names BLATAS and REGINA are embossed in large gold letters on the crimson cloth cover. After Arbit died, I encouraged my family to purchase at auction a Blatas mural that had once hung in the Russian Tea Room, the famous restaurant near Carnegie Hall. It is a scene of the Café de la Paix in Paris, done on Masonite to the exact dimensions of a large banquette near the entrance of the restaurant. I have been told that Arbit painted it in a flourish one night to clear his running tab. The story may be apocryphal – but it sounds like something Arbit might well have done. When the mural was installed in its new location, down the block in the lobby of 130 West Fifty-Seventh Street, a building my family has owned since 1941, I made a special effort to get it suitably framed, and even designed a bronze-plated plaque with Arbit's obituary from the *New York Times*. The article cites a quotation from Arbit about Venice: "The surface of Venice is constantly metamorphosing. Painting Venice is almost like being a restorer, peeling off the layers to find picture after picture underneath."[17]

Regina visits our building from time to time to pay homage to the mural and plaque. Sometimes, she says, it moves her to tears. For me, it was a modest way to express my admiration and gratitude to a friend and mentor.

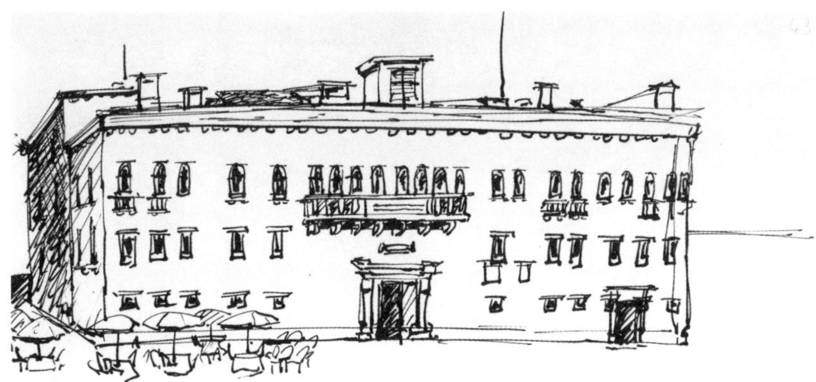

Palazzo Loredan, *1986*

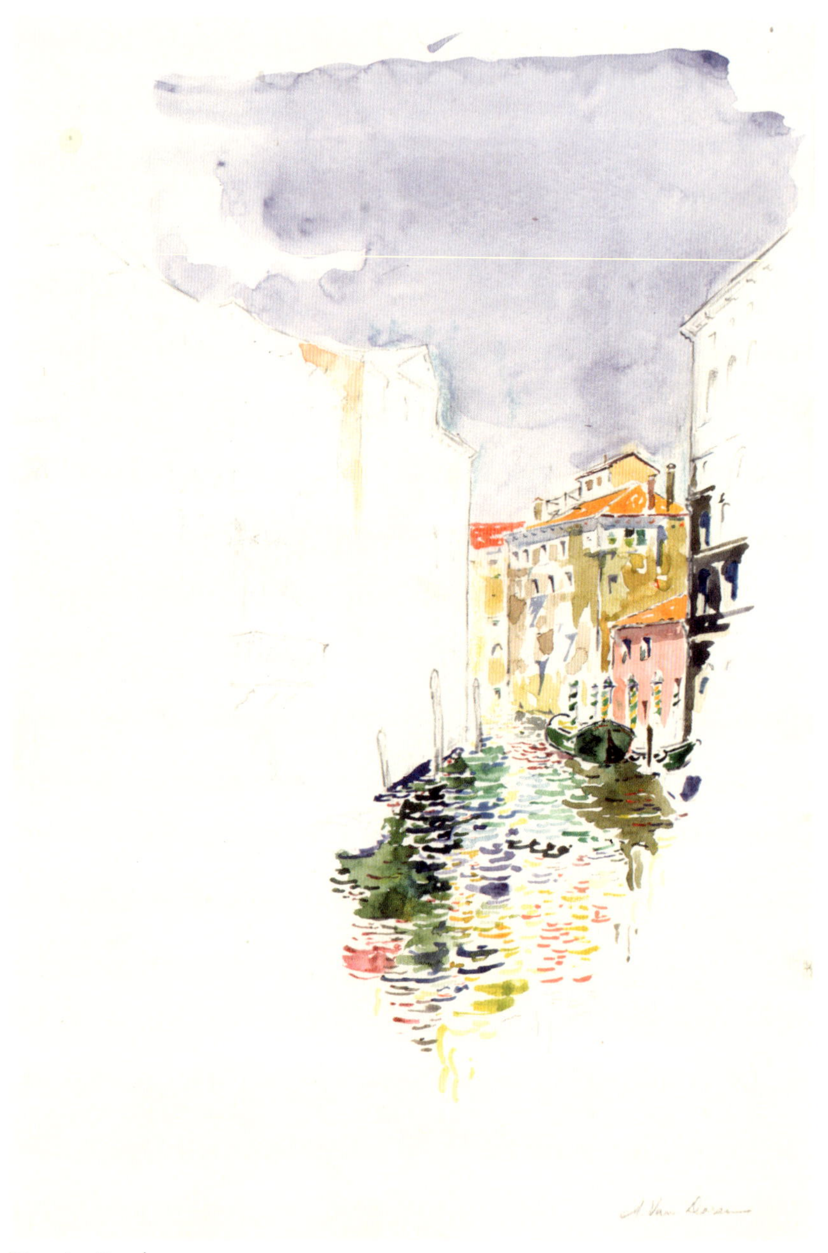

Venetian Canal, *2005*

"Like most painters, I strive for some emotional connection to my subject."

PLEIN AIR MASTERS

He had been selecting his point of view; he took possession of it with a flourish of a pencil. He leaned against a rock, his beautiful little box of watercolors reposed on a ledge of the bank, which showed how inveterately nature ministered to his convenience.

– Henry James[18]

A true testament to Venice is the fact that so many great artists have painted it. It has become a rite of passage, like an actor playing Hamlet. My favorites are J. M. W. Turner, John Singer Sargent, Hercules Brabazon Brabazon, Thomas Moran, and Maurice Prendergast. Walter Sickert, Canaletto, Francesco Guardi, and Richard Parkes Bonington are also exceptional, but the first five share something especially distinctive: they were each masters of watercolor and of painting *en plein air*, or out of doors.

J. M. W. Turner was in a class by himself. His Venetian sketchbooks alone would have made his reputation. I first discovered them in 1987 at the Clore Gallery in London, an annex to the Tate Gallery. The museum had finally opened after years of planning, and I was one of its first visitors. Fortuitously, I had arranged a trip to

England that summer to paint landscapes. I had brought a book, *In the Footsteps of Turner*, which traces his tour of the Lake District. The volume contained several images of his works, accompanied by actual photographs of the sites he painted, and the juxtaposition is revealing: the photos look consistently lifeless compared to what the artist succeeded in bringing forth.

I knew of the Clore because it was reputed to have more than twenty thousand of Turner's watercolors, an astonishing number for any artist. Doing a quick calculation, I figured that Turner needed to paint one every five minutes, over the course of his lifetime, to make this feat remotely possible. How the Clore ended up with so many works is a story in itself. Turner willed his estate in a bequest – one of the largest ever given by an artist – to a trust in England's name with the hope of finding a worthy home for it. Of course things took far longer than expected, as many such well-intentioned efforts invariably do, but architect James Stirling was eventually chosen and the building erected.

My first stop was the Clore's archive department. Climbing the long staircase, its sidewalls decorated in postmodern chic, I entered the main reading room. It was surrounded by shelves of bound folios, stacked one upon the other like ponderous gray bricks. After signing a release, I met the curator, Andrew Wilton. He sat me at a long wooden table and gave me a pair of white gloves. Wilton, who published a 2004 book titled *Turner as Draughtsman*, showed me an inventory of the collection and let me choose what period of Turner's *œuvre* I wanted to see. I requested the series in the Italian Alps, recalling that this was the route Turner took on his way to Venice.

Unwrapping the heavy binders, neatly packed like origami, I carefully sifted through the sketchbooks. Some dated from the late 1700s. As the curator's eyes scrutinized my every move, I was careful not to damage the smooth, laid paper. The edges were soiled and crinkled, evidence of where the artist had held his thumb while he sketched. Touching what Turner had touched was a rare and exhilarating experience.

The watercolors were smaller in size than I had imagined, but not in content. There were views of chasms, gorges, waterfalls, and ravines. Poring over them, it was clear that they were done from life – each scene more death-defying than the last and with a distinct, palpable immediacy Turner must have risked life and limb to render. When I was finished, I asked for the series he painted of Venice. These were familiar views of the city – San Marco, the Rialto, the Giudecca – rendered in Turner's unmistakable style. Color was spare and selective; sky, water, and architecture blended seamlessly. I studied them carefully, hoping to absorb his technique through rapt and reverential osmosis. When the gallery closed, I reluctantly relinquished the watercolors to the curator. Riding home on the Tube, I felt humbled – and depressed. As Manet once exclaimed after seeing a consummate masterwork of Velázquez's, "Why bother to paint at all?"[19]

Joseph Mallord William Turner was born in Covent Garden, London, in 1775, the son of a barber who was so proud of his son he exhibited his work in his shop. (Imagine what the elder would have thought of the recent sale of Turner's *Modern Rome – Campo Vaccino* at Sotheby's for forty-five million dollars!) Turner's mother died young, before her son turned twelve. The young Turner, blessed with an ambition to match his talent, was admitted to the Royal Academy at fourteen, selected by Sir Joshua Reynolds. Originally aspiring to architecture – his dying words were allegedly that he wished he had chosen the profession – he was persuaded by his professors to continue his studies in painting. His passion for buildings never wavered, however, and his early work, especially what I saw at the Met's Turner exhibit in 2007, shows a remarkable facility with architectural detail.

Though revered for his Venetian scenes, Turner – a fleet and nimble draftsman – spent only six weeks in the city over the course of four trips between 1819 and 1840. But his timing was perfect; the city was then rife with the kind of pathos and angst Romantic artists pined for. "Men are we," writes Wordsworth, in his germane 1803 poem, "On the Extinction of the Venetian Republic," "and must grieve when even the Shade/ Of that which once was great is passed away."[20] Venice, having just been defeated by Napoleon, was demoralized and diminished, reduced to a mere parenthesis on the world stage. Turner wasted no time in taking advantage of this plaintive narrative, producing reams of drawings, pastels, oils, and watercolors. His friend William Callow, who witnessed him at work, described him thus: "One evening whilst I was enjoying a cigar in a gondola, I saw in another one Turner sketching San Giorgio, brilliantly lit up by the setting sun. I felt quite ashamed to have idled away the day."[21]

Hercules Brabazon Brabazon (1821–1906), born almost fifty years after Turner, is less well known in the canon, but he is highly prized by connoisseurs for his wispy, often unfinished-looking landscapes. His use of watercolor, the medium he used almost exclusively, is evocative for its power of suggestion and for its liberal use of intense yet understated color. Often light pencil marks are still visible in his pictures, revealing not only the preliminary sketch, but the process by which he worked. The artist's bodacious name, which is repeated (he was originally born Hercules Brabazon Sharpe), has no doubt helped perpetuate his reputation, but his work stands alone. A great friend of Sargent, who painted a portrait of him, Brabazon was reared in a wealthy English family, and became recognized as a legitimate artist only late in life. He didn't exhibit until he was seventy, and not until he was persuaded by Sargent, who reappears often in his biography as a lasting influence. Both men respected each other's work unconditionally, and it's not unheard of for curators to mistake one for the other. Brabazon's watercolors, in general, such as *A View of the Piazzetta*, are breezier, less detailed, and less controlled – their palette resembles the exuberant blues of Bonington's more than

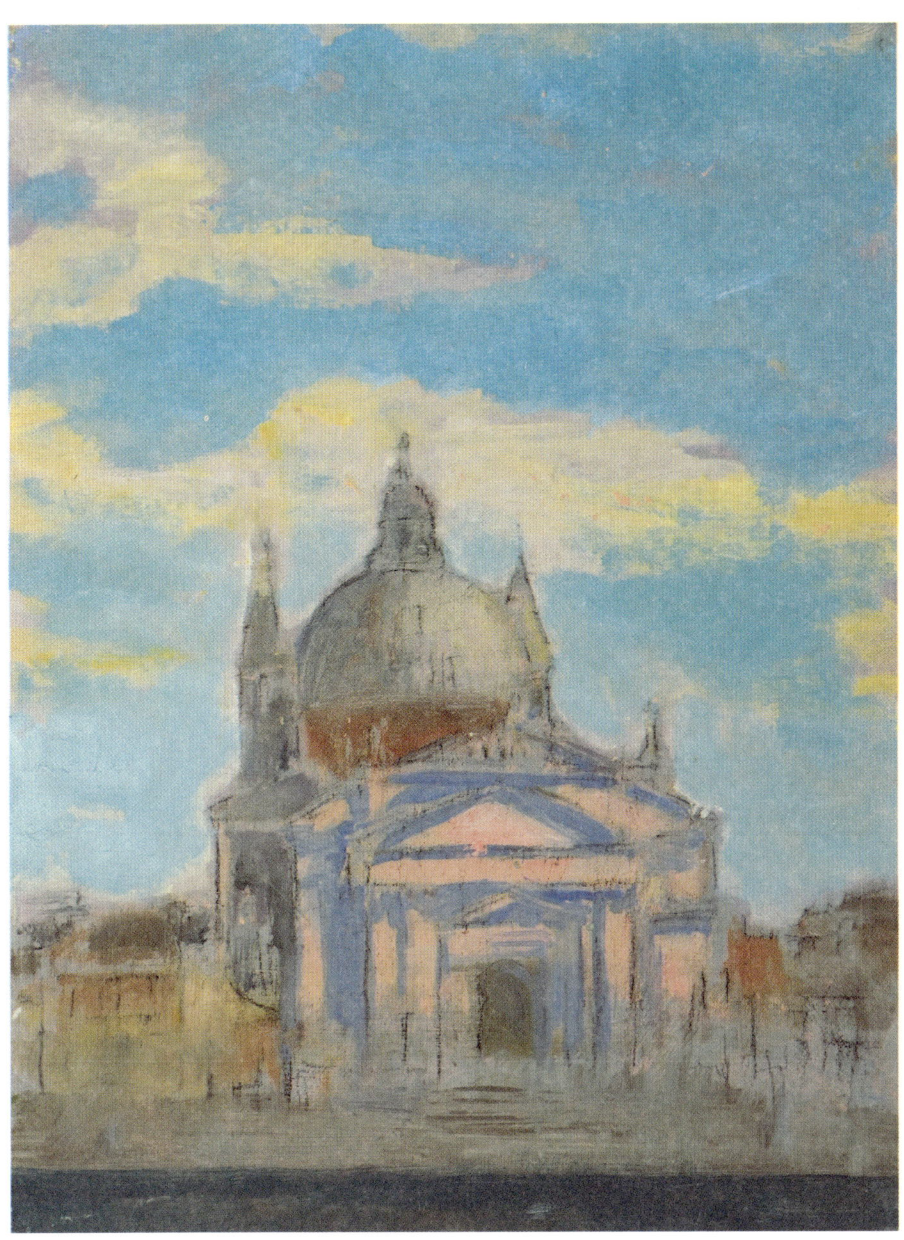

Il Redentore, *2010*

Sargent's – but there is a scintillating like-minded luminosity to both these painters.

A friend of mine, Jessica Tcherpedine, a botanical artist who lives in New York, once gave me the chance to see an original Brabazon. She owns a small watercolor that hangs in her living room on Park Avenue, part of a modest but handsome art collection. When she invited me to see it in November 2009, I leapt at the prospect. Few know who Brabazon was, let alone own one of his works. Jessica's small picture, a vignette of a Venetian doorway, was given to her by her father years ago, when she was still in her teens. She chose between two of the artist's works. In retrospect she wishes she had selected the other one, a landscape, but I assured her she had done well.

Born in Paris, Brabazon originally studied mathematics at Cambridge before training to be a lawyer. Over his lifetime, he traveled widely and often, recording his trips in watercolor. Besides Sargent, his circle of distinguished friends included Franz Liszt. When he first exhibited, Ruskin praised his work. Others followed, and the English art critic Sir Frederick Wedmore described Brabazon as "a country gentleman, who at seventy years old made his debut as a professional artist, and straightaway became famous."[22] But Brabazon was taken with the beauty of color from an early age, and enjoyed painting flowers when he was a boy. One account records how he loved to hold a ruby of his mother's, staring at it for hours to watch how the light changed within. He was a natural observer and wrote an eighty-page diary when he was only twelve, entitled "A Tour in Germany," which included many of his drawings. Eventually, after growing disenchanted with the law, Brabazon persuaded his father to let him study art in Rome for three years. When he inherited the family fortune, he took the opportunity to paint as much as possible over the next fifty years. Never considering himself more than a serious amateur, he often gave his drawings away to friends, and when he won critical acclaim, it made not the slightest difference. He was simply happy doing what he loved most.

Brabazon's friend, John Singer Sargent (1856–1925), needs perhaps little introduction. With the exception of Turner, he is the greatest watercolorist of Venice. Precocious as a youth, like Brabazon (his childhood sketchbooks are the work of an already mature artist), Sargent lived mostly in Europe, though his parents were American. He studied his craft both in Florence and Paris, and at the École des Beaux-Arts, to which, because of his American heritage, he was only reluctantly admitted. He dazzled his instructors with his raw talent, while leaving his peers intensely envious. Sargent was arguably one of the finest draftsmen of his era, and got better as he got older. Excelling magnificently at portraiture, like the Renaissance artists he admired, Sargent could paint anything, and did.

I've loved Sargent ever since I first saw his scenes of Venice at the Metropolitan Museum in New York in the late eighties. Happily, I got the chance to see them again in 2007 at the Adelson Gallery, just down the street from the museum. Warren Adelson, the proprietor and a leading collector of nineteenth-century American art, gave me a preview before the opening. Some of the images in the exhibit were new to me, including a dozen half-finished works that a museum might not consider worth hanging. It was edifying to view them all together as an ensemble. I noted Sargent's supreme confidence with color. Bold strokes of yellow ocher and burnt sienna were applied with vigor, even brashness. Gondolas boldly rendered in deep ivory black heaved in water saturated with thalo blue and viridian. Sargent was fearless. There were lessons to be learned here, and I took mental notes despite the crush of patrons who elbowed their way in front of me. I was not surprised to learn that the pictures in this series, some of them with titles like *The Dogana* and *View of the Grand Canal*, were among the painter's personal favorites. After he quit portraiture, Sargent devoted his last years almost entirely to watercolor. He could stomach only so many of the relentless demands made by spoiled patrons to make their faces more attractive than they actually were.

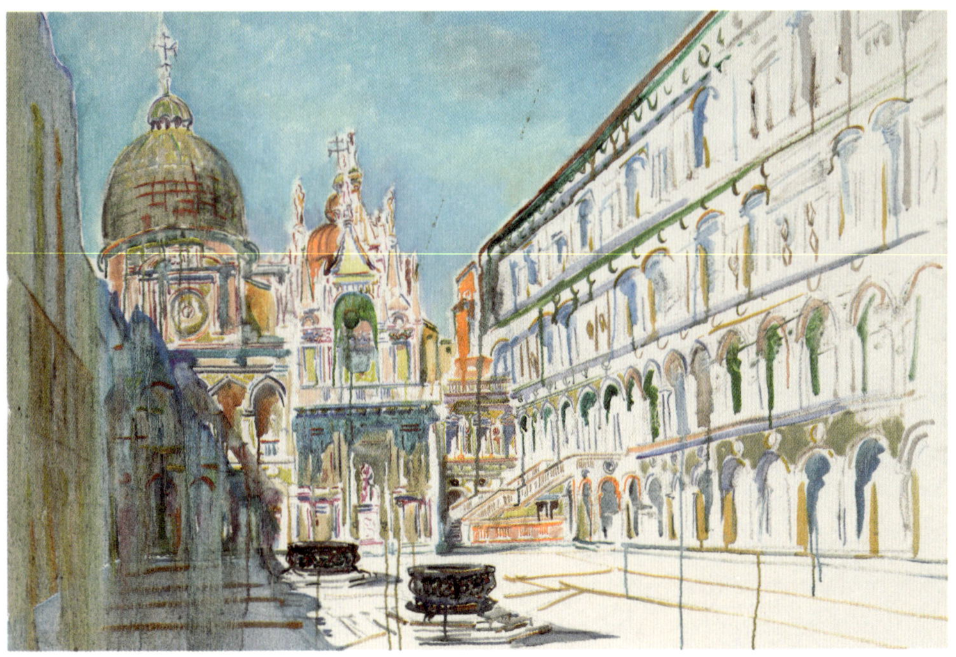

Palazzo Ducale Courtyard in Sun, *2011*

Sargent loved painting architecture, and nowhere is this more evident than in his studies of the Santa Maria della Salute in Venice. He produced many versions of the church, each from a different angle, and they are all small masterpieces. Often their compositions are cropped, isolating a particular portion of the building that interested him. He found endless inspiration in this baroque structure, and did some oils of it as well. Watercolor, in short, was an intensely liberating medium for Sargent. I sense that freedom whenever I see the photographs of him painting outdoors. He is dressed like a member of the Alpine border patrol, in hiking boots and hat, sitting on a stool on the hillside with an umbrella (for shade, not rain) pitched in the ground. Although his demeanor seems grave – his posture is upright and stiff – there is little doubt of the creative giddiness inside him.

My former art teacher at the National Academy in New York, Reeve Schley, was a great exponent of outdoor painting. A distinguished artist himself, Schley felt that this was the only way to see bona fide color. He loved braving the elements and did so with Hemingwayesque bravado. Watching Schley paint, with a gathering storm overhead, was an education in itself: he brandished a large, floppy hat and a sturdy easel that he stuck firmly in the ground. He kept his gear light: a small Windsor Newton palette box, brushes wrapped in a Chinese mat, and an assortment of Arches watercolor blocks. As the wind picked up, he kept his cool. He seemed not to worry that his picture was about to blow away, demonstrating the trick of balancing brushes and palette with one hand, while painting with the other. (Degas hated this method of working outdoors, declaring that painting is not a sport.) He often cited Winslow Homer, who had an epiphany in the Bahamas in 1879, discovering how color in the brightest sunlight was also at its most intense – the opposite of what an amateur artist might assume. Watching the natives fishing in the ocean, Homer meticulously observed how the sun illuminated their pitch-black hair and brown bodies with deep, rich hues.

The late David Levine, another great watercolorist, was also among my teachers. When he was not painting *en plein air* – his method of choice – he was conducting an informal art class, The Painting Group, which he founded with fellow artist Aaron Shikler. This weekly atelier, which emphasizes figurative painting, started in 1954 and has met every Wednesday for the last fifty years. I have been a member for an instructive and rewarding twenty, and during most of that time I've had a front-row seat, watching how Levine worked. After arranging the pose, he always began by applying washes onto a Strathmore board, laying in a rough sketch that formed his background. (This technique of preparing a "ground" has been used for centuries, but not often with watercolor.) After these washes dried, his sure fingers moved quickly and with precision. He filled in shadows first; then, through a series of improvised scrapings and stumpings (a method of using a sponge to pull up layers of color from the painting surface), he "worked" the thin board over the course of several hours, even days, until an image emerged. Levine, who died in 2009, was also a celebrated caricaturist, and his sense of line reminds me of Honoré Daumier, the great nineteenth-century French political cartoonist whom he worshipped. Both had the same biting wit and love of humanity, which comes across in their portrayal of unforgettable characters, especially judges and statesmen. Though he produced many fine works from this class, Levine preferred working outside. His frequent subject was Coney Island, and he made countless studies of the old amusement park, and especially of the regular beachgoers who fill the boardwalk. At Levine's memorial, our mutual friend Byron Dobell recalled: "David liked to say that important artists held nothing back, stopped at nothing to knock the viewer out. What a privilege it was for us to be around during his lifetime."[23]

Levine also loved Venice, and he made pilgrimages to the city every few years to paint it. Even as an older man suffering from various ailments, he made the long trip. When I asked him whether he could work from photographs, he replied (I might have guessed), "Nope. *Being* in Venice is the only way I can paint it. The same goes for Brooklyn." He wanted to feel the air, hear the sounds, smell the sea – get it in his blood. An aspiring artist might wonder how these sensations really help *seeing?* The answer is simple: inspiration. That intangible quality, which varies significantly from person to person, must be present. This may sound overly precious, but it's true. Like most painters, I strive for some emotional connection to my subject; that's what drives me. But it can be elusive. Often it's buried in my subconscious, linked with some person or place from long ago. Sometimes it's as subtle as the way sunlight enters a room at the end of the day. My grandfather Mark Van Doren, the Pulitzer Prize–winning poet, wrote "This Amber Sunstream" about this effect:

No living man in any western room
But sits at amber sunset round a tomb.[24]

Yet as hard as inspiration is to find, it is harder to keep. It is as fickle as a mood. I am also easily susceptible to distraction: some bad news, a phone call, a lost set of keys can thoroughly derail me. There's no use in resisting. Sometimes it is better to just run around the block, play the banjo, or eat an éclair to get back "in the zone," as my son, Henry, likes to say of NFL quarterbacks when they hit their stride. For some painters, this productive state can be realized by using photographs. But working from a 4 × 6 glossy just doesn't do it for me. I would rather work from memory, or from a sketch in my notebook, than be seduced by an image made by a machine.

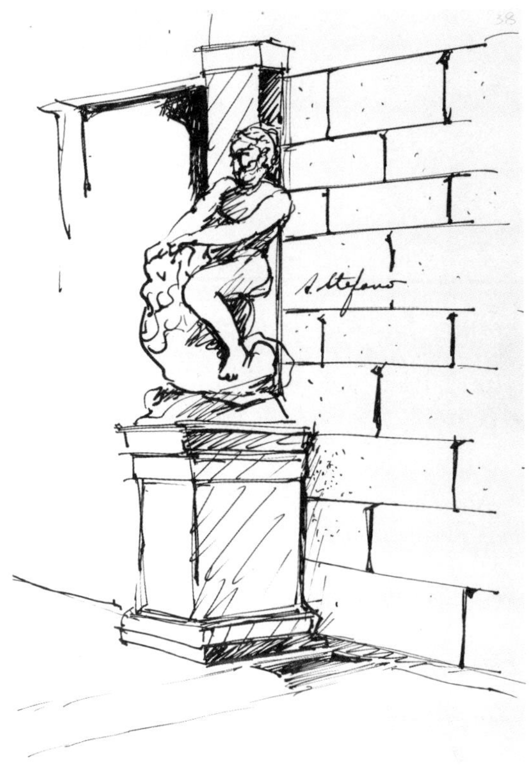

Entry to Palazzo Pisani, *1986*

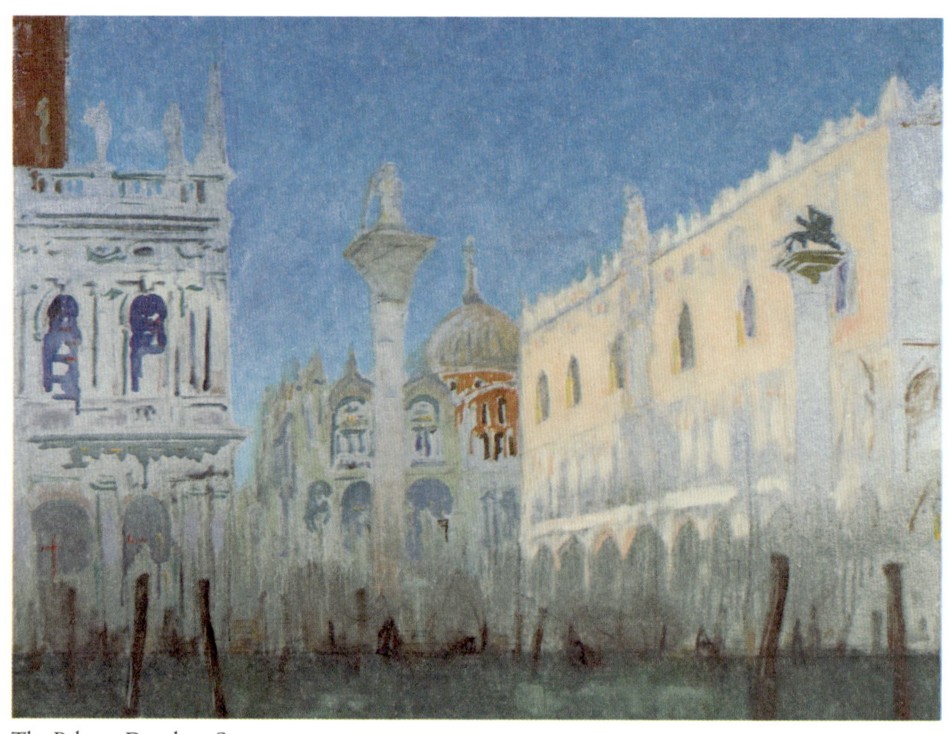

The Palazzo Ducale at Sunset, *2010*

"San Marco has an attendant, no less important distinction: it is, quite simply, a great place to sketch."

BYZANTINE DREAM

It was a great Piazza, as I thought, anchored,
like all the rest, in the deep ocean. On its
broad bosom, was a palace, more majestic
and magnificent in its old age, than all
the buildings of the earth . . . and . . .
a cathedral, gorgeous in the wild
luxuriant fancies of the East.

– Charles Dickens [25]

Piazza San Marco, to cite a famous cliché, has been often called the greatest drawing room in Europe. And while this was once true, it is no more. The days of waiting at Florian for the train from Paris are over, as English historian John Julius Norwich laments in *Venice in Old Photographs.*[26] Drawing rooms suggest a certain decorum, the air of a salon, and these have been replaced by polyester shorts and Nike T-shirts. But San Marco is still the heart of Venice, and the city would be lost without it. So would I. Street signs for the Piazza are everywhere – an attempt by the civic authorities to prevent mass mazeophobia – and while most markers are well-intentioned, some seem sadistically placed to lead tourists, like me, further astray. Yet I manage. At times I've tried to avoid the square altogether – the crowds can be oppressive, to say the least – but it requires Magellan-like navigation to do so. Side streets fan out like octopus tentacles in all directions, and I find myself walking in circles only to return to the place from which I set forth.

I think of San Marco as the Central Park of Venice: it is the largest open space in the city and, undeniably, its soul. I wonder whether its original architects foresaw their creation as a masterpiece of urban planning. Scholars invariably list Piazza San Marco as among the greatest public spaces of Europe. Hugh Honour, author of *The Companion Guide to Venice*, wrote, "It is one only of a few great city squares that retains a feeling of animation even when there are few people in it."[27] Its scheme includes an ingenious optical effect: one of the side buildings, now the Museo Correr, is pivoted outward at a slight angle, accentuating the perspective and creating the illusion of a much larger square. (This architectural idea is similarly adopted to great effect at Capitoline Hill in Rome and Lincoln Center in New York.) The Piazza also acts as a natural portal to Venice, welcoming its visitors like conquering heroes of yore. Arriving by boat from the airport, I know of no more welcoming site in the world.

Beyond its lofty role as the epicenter of Venice, San Marco has an attendant, no less important distinction: it is, quite simply, a great place to sketch. Despite pigeons, concessionaires, and tour guides, I can always find a quiet spot to draw. Like a great estate, there are places to spread out (the base of St. Mark's column), spots for shade (the colonnade of San Silvestre), and corners for solitude (the courtyard of the Palazzo Ducale). And if I don't mind an audience, I can place my easel smack in the middle of the square. The cafés provide pleasant background music, and the gossiping *grandes dames* add local color. I lean back as I paint and enjoy the show: the flags, the Basilica, the clock tower. And when the men in bronze strike at the top of the hour, it's time "to homeward plod, my weary way."[28] Like Venice itself, the Basilica of San Marco ripens and mellows with age. The church could use a good cleaning, but its allure remains its antiquity. It does not need to reinvent itself, as so many buildings of an advanced age today are compelled to do, especially in New York, where the current rage is recladding them in glass. San Marco is simply a nonpareil: like no other building in the world, its structure has been added to over the centuries, making it peerless and inimitable. It is a great jumble of Byzantine, Gothic, Renaissance, and Moorish styles; the architectural equivalent, at first glance, of a train wreck. Yet underlying these seemingly incongruous parts, some of which date to the eleventh century, a rigorous order and symmetry emerges. The primary entrance is set directly on an axis with the center of the Piazza, and the main doors are flanked by equidistant columns, set in groups to form the base of the structure. The upper story takes its cue from the lower one, echoing its curvilinear geometry both in the clerestory openings and in the onion domes, which Ruskin, in his *Stones of Venice*, likens to Tartar helmets.[29] In the end, the building's eclectic style is a perfect marriage between the East and West; and Venice, situated on the Adriatic, is historically the hinge between these two worlds.

One of the little rituals I observe when I arrive in Venice (after making a reservation at my favorite restaurant, Locanda Montin, which has a trellised garden) is to head straight for San Marco, to get reacquainted. I invariably see things I've never noticed before. The Basilica is a mélange of impressive relics, many looted from Constantinople and the Hippodrome during the Crusades; and each – including the four bronze horses and the sculpture of the Tetrarchs – has found its way onto the façade like a Joseph Cornell shadow box. Its interior is equally dramatic, and worth the long queue to see. What astonishes one at first is how cavernous the space is. Judging from its exterior, it is hard to tell how large the Basilica really is; the façade is merely the stage curtain before the opera begins. Upon entering the nave, it's impossible to miss the incredible, shimmering mosaics on the ceiling, set in a sea of gold. (Hagia Sophia, the magnificent Byzantine church I visited in Istanbul in 1991, was less of a surprise: its exterior and interior are equally massive.) The nineteenth-century artists Walter Sickert and Maurice Prendergast are among the many painters who have made beautiful studies of this remarkable space. "There are usually three or four painters with their easel," as Henry James remarked in 1882, "set up in uncertain equilibrium, on the undulating floor."[30]

The Basilica, the actual repository for the remains of Saint Mark, routinely shows "good face," to borrow a phrase from the fashion industry, and its rich array of colors, handsomely displayed on the marble columns and capitals, is a pleasure to draw. One late afternoon, trudging back to my hotel after a day of painting, I took a shortcut through Piazza San Marco, toward the Fenice opera house, now fully rebuilt after nearly burning to the ground in 1998. When I was halfway across the Piazza, I felt something tug at my back. Turning, I beheld the purest ephemera: the last of the summer sun was spreading streaks of gold across the western face of the Basilica, illuminating the mosaics with a burnished flame. Hardly in the mood to work more that day, I nevertheless recognized an opportunity. Summoning a second wind, I pulled out my materials, set up my easel, and worked till twilight.

San Marco Basilica, however, is not to everyone's taste. Some think it looks like the Creature from the Black Lagoon and Mark Twain once called it a "warty bug on a meditative walk."[31] But I consider these assessments complimentary, for if a building like this resembles something organic, it is honorific. I never have been one for the machine age in architecture, nor in painting for that matter; glass boxes leave me cold as does the Dutch artist Mondrian's work, which looks more like graphic exercise than painting. I simply don't think a building needs to look like a turbine or a toaster to be aesthetically pleasing.

My grandmother Lydia, a talented artist who studied painting in Germany, loved to draw San Marco. She was best at pastels and colored pencils, and I admired how she included people in her drawings, something I find difficult to do. (It is hard enough to render a detailed building, let alone add squiggly figures that don't stand still). I remember watching my grandmother work when I traveled on vacation with her; I was ten and we stayed in Venice for two weeks. As we passed the time in cafés overlooking the Piazza, she routinely pulled out her sketchbook – one with a marbleized cover she kept in her Gucci handbag – and began to sketch. In no time, or so it seemed, she produced several small but engaging pictures, often including my grandfather in the background. Usually he was hidden behind a copy of the *International Herald Tribune*, but she always managed to get one side of his head, his white shock of hair sticking up. She worked fast, and encouraged me to do the same. I was tentative and my fingers labored to keep up. When she finished, she neatly tucked her sketches back into her purse, without much fanfare. Forty years later, they hang in frames in her old living room on West Fifty-Seventh Street in New York. She died in 2003, but her apartment is still in the family, and I was pleased to see the sketches recently on her wall, alive and well, and beautiful in physical fact and memory.

Lydia also made several studies of the Palazzo Ducale, next to San Marco. Though less ornate, this building, designed in the style of a huge palazzo, is no less appealing than the Basilica. It is not a house of worship, nor does it try to be. It is in fact the largest secular building in Venice. Majestic but unimposing, it is essentially a residence – not of a monarch, but of an elected official. The home of more than fifty doges since 1343, the Palazzo Ducale has also led a double life: it is a sort of Venetian incarnation of Dr. Jekyll and Mr. Hyde. It was a benevolent House of State, symbol of the longest continuous republic in the world, and also a house of horrors, with torture chambers hidden throughout the basement. The Bridge of Sighs is the symbol of this duality (as Lord Byron once wrote, "I stood on the Bridge of Sighs: A palace and a prison"[32]), its handsome stone exterior contrasting with the inherent gloom inside, where condemned prisoners saw freedom for the last time when they crossed the canal to meet their fateful end.

A long colonnade wraps around the entire lower story of the Palazzo Ducale, giving it the appearance of weightlessness. This serves two additional purposes: it casts upon the citizenry some shade from the sun and it creates a play of solids and voids that just ask to be painted. Above the row of thick columns, a long line of circular, cloverleaf windows spread across the façade, like a procession in one of Gentile Bellini's paintings of the doge's entourage. The inlaid tiles on the walls above are reminiscent of Persian design, suggesting an Oriental carpet. Deborah Howard in her book *The Architectural History of Venice*, sums up: "It's almost as if an early type of lagoon house raised on wooden stiles has been petrified like a coral on the seashore."[33] If Giovanni Mocenigo, the fifteenth-century doge, were miraculously to return, he would probably think nothing had changed.

At the corner of the Palazzo Ducale, next to the Bibliotheca Marciana by Jacopo Sansovino, two fifty-foot-high columns – built centuries ago – stand side by side facing the lagoon. Each has a statue atop its capital: the lion of Saint Mark's on the one and Saint Theodore on the other. Both landmarks triumphantly mark the entrance to the Piazzeta, or Little Piazza, which is the smaller of the two squares that comprise San Marco. Each column has a story to tell. Of Theodore we know this: he was considered the first patron saint of Venice (before the relics of Saint Mark were brought to the city in 828 A.D.) and the doge's original chapel was thought to have been dedicated to him. Theodore's claim to fame was that he defiantly resisted the persecution of Christians in the city of Heraclea Pontica, in modern-day Turkey, and was crucified as a result. Miraculously, he survived. But like a true martyr, he was eventually beheaded. Today he poses high above Venice, a long staff in one hand and a shield in another. A crocodile, the animal with which he is often associated, lies subdued at his feet. In the Middle Ages, renditions of this column and its neighbor appeared prominently in illuminated manuscripts, their renderings often towering – disproportionately – over the Basilica and the Palazzo Ducale.

Though Theodore has a secure place in Venetian history, it is the lion of Saint Mark's that has greater claim as the city's mascot. It has become Venice's unofficial coat of arms. The proud beast is traditionally illustrated with one front paw raised upward, steadying an open book inscribed with the text *Pax tibi, Marce, Evangelista meus* ("Peace be upon you, O Mark, my Evangelist"). The lion has long been a symbol of this saint – whose remains were smuggled from Constantinople in the eleventh century – and images of it abound in Venice and its environs. In fact, it is not unheard of to see bas-reliefs as far away as Crete, a former Venetian colony. Souvenir shops on the Rialto bridge are full of replicas, and even winners at the Venice Film Festival receive a so-called Golden Lion. Jan Morris wrote of this famous feline: "They [the Venetians] built him onto their corbels, they slipped him into their allegories, they stuck him on gateposts, they made him the corner-stones of bridges. Citizens kept live lions in their gardens, and for a time a State Lion lived in a golden cage in the Piazza."[34]

It's ironic that this icon was a symbol of peace (*Pax tibi, Marce*), given how historically bellicose Venice was. The city was perennially at war for four hundred years – Milan and Genoa being its principal adversaries – and it is only because Venice is surrounded by marshes and shallow water that invaders didn't prevail. Naval battles such as the 1571 Battle of Lepanto against the Ottomans were its specialty and at one time the armada was without equal. I've often wondered, therefore, how Venice ever had time to produce as much art as it did. Guns, ships, and cannons, maybe – but not Titians, Tintorettos, or Bellinis. The historian Theodore Rabb questions the origins of Venice's nickname, La Serenissima, in a recent essay: "One readily concedes that here is the most serene of republics. But nothing could be further from the truth. There is no place on earth whose fate and achievements owe more to fierce hostilities, to bitter competition, to ruthless struggles for survival and supremacy."[35] It seems to me that calling Venice Sparta might have been more appropriate. But perhaps therein lies an explanation: the Venetians' impulse behind such a beautiful city – a fantasy, if you will – was the desire to create something as far removed from grim reality as possible.

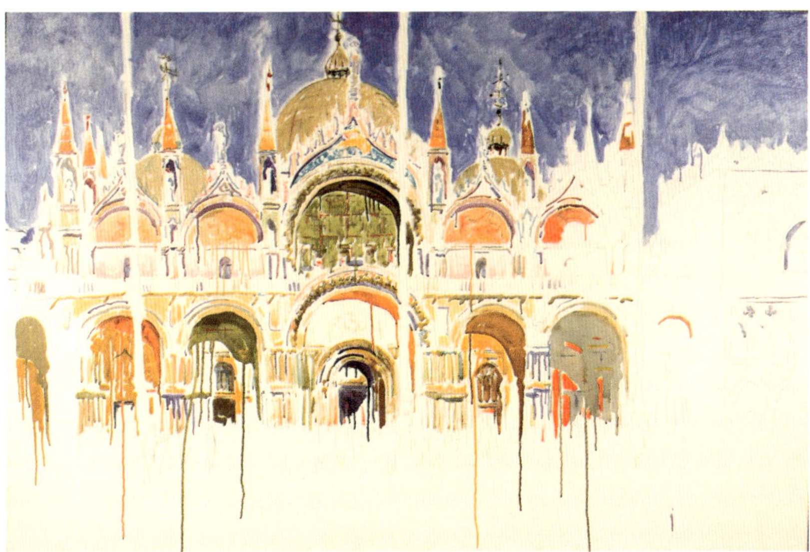

Exterior of the Basilica, *2009*

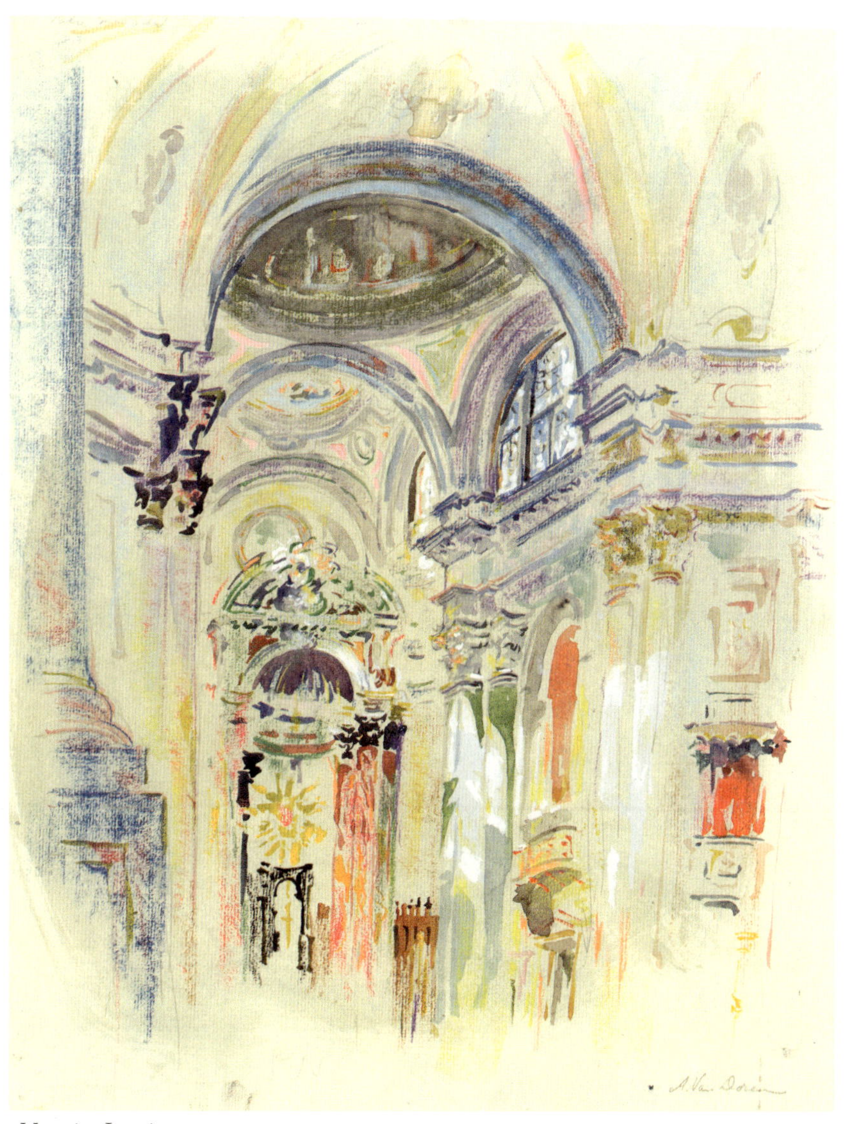

Venetian Interior, *2005*

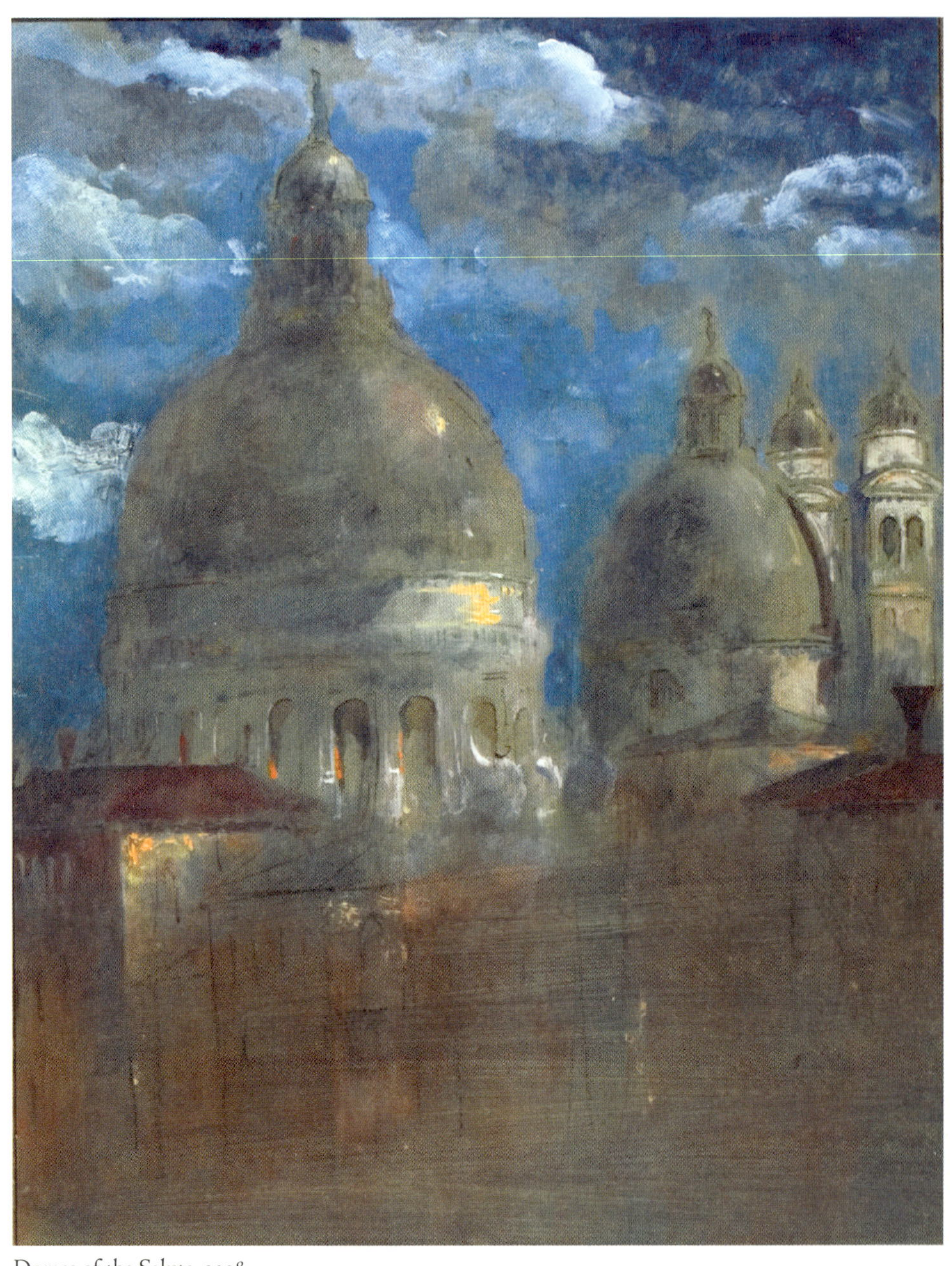

Domes of the Salute, *2008*

“The story behind the Salute, which took more than fifty years to build, reads like a fairy tale.”

LONGHENA'S MIRACLE

With its eight sides facing eight winds,
like the Tower of Winds in Athens,
[the Salute] serves as an inspiration
to Venetian seafarers.

– Deborah Howard [36]

Venice, it is fair to say, is esteemed less for its individual buildings than for the cumulative montage of its architecture, its waterways, and its turbulent history. To this, the church of Santa Maria Salute is a glorious exception. Perched at the southern tip of the Dorsoduro, this great domed vision, completed in 1680, frames the entrance to the Grand Canal, and with great ceremony. It is a masterpiece of baroque architecture and one of the few Venetian examples of this style, of which Rome has so many. Huge columns and elaborate scrollwork rise from its ornate exterior, twisting and turning like the limbs of Poseidon. Statues of angels, perched above the main doors, guard the entrance. John Ruskin once said that the effect was enough "to raise one from the gates of Death."[37] The Salute, for all its size, is not nearly so big as Christopher Wren's greatest church, St. Paul's in London, or the Panthéon in Paris by Jacques-Germain Soufflot. But in Venice, where the scale is much smaller, the Salute is formidable. Like the wedge-shaped Flatiron Building in New York, it triumphantly anchors the end of a long triangular piece of land. Its bronze doors, faded to a rich patina, are large enough to embrace not only the Doge but also the Pope and the Holy Trinity. Venetians from all quarters covet their views of it, but the Accademia Bridge offers the best perspective. From the Grand Canal, the Salute stands like the bow of an enormous ship, its steps descending to the water's edge like a flowing cape. Remarkably, this building floats entirely on water: one hundred and sixty thousand wooden stakes, or *pilotti*, form its foundation. This construction method, dating from the eleventh century, is essential for a city built entirely upon mud. Just beyond the church, the gold sphere atop Dogana di Mare, the old Customs House, radiates in the sunlight and forms an arresting backdrop – a symbol of the maritime commerce and conquest that made Venice an empire. Of all the Italian city-states of the Renaissance, the Venetian Republic was by far the most important trading and sea power, with emissaries in every major port in Europe. Its commercial empire stretched from Padua to Crete, and when its mercantile fleet would return to the Grand Canal after yet another profitable voyage, Santa Maria della Salute welcomed them on the horizon.

The story behind the Salute, which took more than fifty years to build, reads like a fairy tale. In 1630, following the end of yet another plague – it seems that Venice's population was routinely wiped out every hundred years – the Doge decreed that a building be erected in honor of the Virgin Mary. A competition was announced, and several prominent architects participated. Eleven submissions were received, including plans by some of the leading practitioners of the day – Matteo Ignoli, Alessandro Varotari, and Berteo Belli – but only two made the final round. When the jury reached its decision, the choice stunned everyone – except perhaps the winner, Baldassare Longhena.

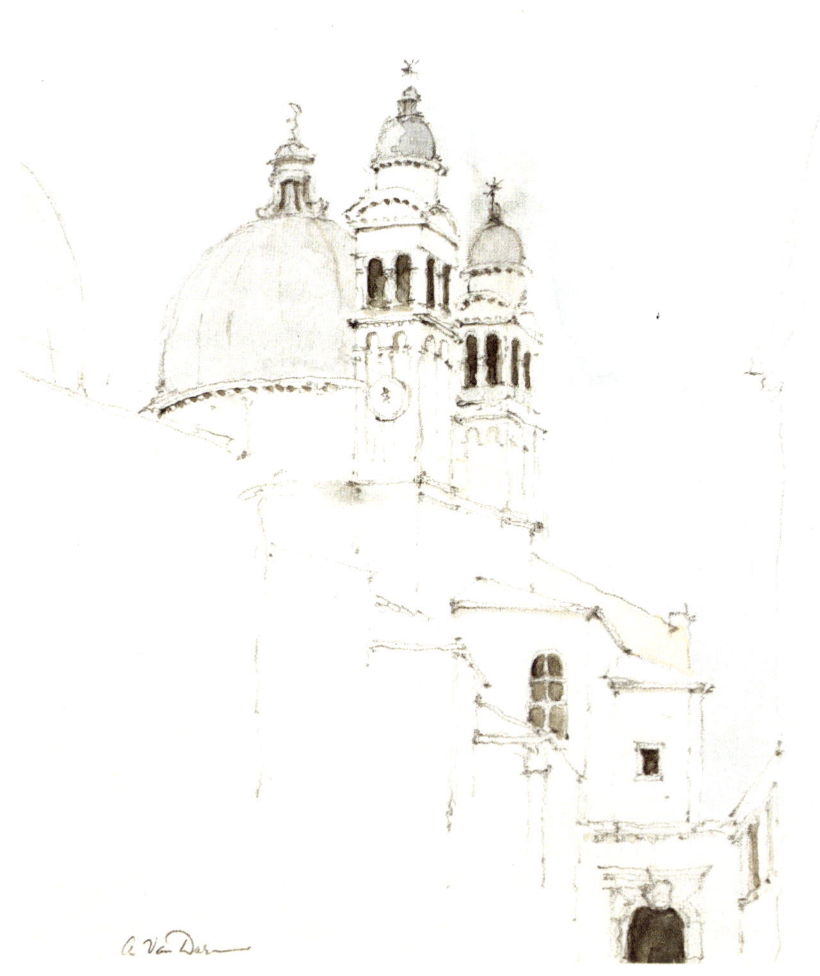

The Salute, *1986*

A young architect with few commissions to his credit, Longhena, then only twenty-six, was thought to be too inexperienced to solve such a complex engineering problem, let alone carry it through to completion. The final tally by the Senate was sixty-six in favor, twenty-nine opposed, with two abstentions. But when the losers cried foul, they did so more out of jealousy than any judiciousness: Longhena's winning concept, which he likened to a vast revolving machine, was brilliant, and they secretly wished they had concocted it themselves. Longhena later wrote: "I have created a church in the form of a rotunda, a work of new invention, never before built in Venice."[38] Among the few proposals that survive, Antonio Smeraldi's is much more conventional, and largely derivative of early churches in Venice such as the Redentore and San Giorgio Maggiore, both designed by Andrea Palladio. Another design, by Varotari, is mostly conceptual and not fully realized enough to be a serious contender. Longhena's scheme is not only original, including a centralized octagonal plan for the site, but it is also thoroughly conceived, down to the last detail, including structural specifications and a budget. No doubt this impressed the judges. Perhaps Longhena had already foreseen his place in history.

Born in Venice in 1598, Baldassare Longhena studied with the architect Vincenzo Scamozzi and later completed some of his mentor's works, such as the Procuatie Nuove in San Marco. Known for his short stature (even by the standards of the day) and his penchant for black dress, Longhena was the son of a stonemason who came from Lake Lugano, where another baroque master, Borromini, was also raised. The younger Longhena also designed Chiesa dell'Ospedaletto and Santa Maria degli Scalzi, and he was christened "Il Nuovo Palladio" by the poet Franceschi.

I especially enjoy drawing the Salute from the Hotel Gritti Palace *traghetto* stop, near Harry's Bar, a favorite of Hemingway's, though this is not without its perils. The ferry landing is tiny, and has a small dock for gondolas transporting passengers across the canal. People stumble out of the boat every fifteen minutes, routinely knocking over my paint and brushes, indifferent to the chaos. No sooner do I clean up than another gondola arrives and the cycle repeats. Out of necessity, or perhaps desperation, I try to finish my pictures faster. It is a frenetic exercise but yields interesting results, and trumps procrastination.

Rendering the Salute can be daunting, and the dome is particularly difficult to draw accurately. Since it is much larger relative to the rest of the structure – unusual for a classical building – I tend to make the dome too small. More often than not, domes on traditional buildings are less prominent and generally set back from the main façade, though there are exceptions such as the Capitol in Washington or Les Invalides in Paris, where Napoleon is buried. Seeking inspiration, I consulted Turner and also Thomas Moran, the great American artist, to see how *they* painted the Salute. Surprisingly, their proportions were generally off the mark: they either made the dome too tall or too narrow. Was it artistic license, or did they work from memory? Either way, I was not convinced till I turned to Canaletto (1697–1768), Venice's greatest scene painter. His works are so detailed you could reconstruct the entire city with them, and scholars speculate that Canaletto (originally named Antonio Canal) used a *camera obscura* – a novel Renaissance device for generating perspective – to make his pictures. Others say Venice was simply in his blood; he lived there most of his life and continued his legacy by passing on his technique to his nephew, Bernardo Bellotto, whose works rival his uncle's, especially his cityscapes of Berlin and Warsaw.

In quest of Canaletto, I headed to the Accademia, near the wooden bridge of the same name, which houses Venice's great art collection. Oddly enough, I found only one of his paintings, and it was not even a scene of Venice, but an academic work he did to earn his degree from art school. I retraced my steps through four floors, but found nothing. Were they on loan for an exhibition? Or was there a separate museum dedicated to his work? It was disheartening to say the least; it felt like the time I'd raced to see the Pantheon in Rome only to find it closed indefinitely, buried under scaffolding. When I feebly asked a guard whether the Canalettos might be in storage, his broken English and my garbled Italian collided in midair like glue and gnocchi. Finally, the receptionist solved the mystery: the majority of the artist's works are in England. He was a favorite of the British aristocracy, especially the Duke of Bedford, who had purchased hundreds of his works over the decades and had shrewdly lured him there to paint views of London. Disappointed, I went to a bookstore nearby and bought a monograph of Canaletto's work. Sure enough, on the second page I found his painting entitled *The Grand Canal and the Church of the Salute*. I felt validated: his proportions were dead on, and I was now confident how to approach my own rendering.

I have also tried to paint the interior of the Salute, which is no easy task. One afternoon I made a valiant attempt. The church was empty, and thinking I had the place to myself, I sat in awe of the geometry that is so hard to appreciate in photographs. I was about to lay in some color for the massive columns when a woman who worked at the postcard stand approached. She informed me that I was not allowed to work inside the church without permission from her superior (who, of course, was out to lunch). I pleaded my case, explaining that I was almost finished, but she wouldn't budge. I could have been the reincarnation of Doge Loredan it seemed, but to no avail. After waiting for an hour and attempting to add a few surreptitious brushstrokes, I gave up and dropped the case. Once home, I finished the rest from memory, and pinned it to the wall of my *pensione*. The picture was not as complete as I'd hoped, but it accomplished what I wanted: a memento of the moment I shared with an architectural masterpiece.

Once a year (or thereabouts) at an arts club in Manhattan, I meet for dinner with a group of friends, loosely assembled as "lovers of Venice." Bill Dean, the organizer of this casual soirée, is a lawyer and essayist who visits Venice once a year (where he is a regular at the Hotel Seguso). His only requirement for our evening is that the participants present one anecdote about La Serenissima. We are all unapologetic Venetophiles – a species of which I am proud to belong – and guiltlessly swap fulsome clichés and expound sugary epithets about our favorite city. Seated at a long table with two large candelabras at either end, Dean, a tall patrician figure, presides, while a sumptuous feast of authentic Venetian dishes is served: pasta with beans, salted whitefish with polenta, steak with Parmesan cheese and balsamic vinegar, or green gnocchetti with smoked ham and mushrooms. During the dinner we take turns making presentations; topics have included Titian's *Assumption* at Chiesa di Santa Maria dei Frari, William Dean Howells's *Venetian Life*, and the origins of Ca' Pesaro, Venice's museum of modern art. Once I took the opportunity to ask the guests which was their favorite building in Venice. Without hesitation, most of them said the Salute. To them it was not only a beautiful church, but also illustrative and iconic of the city as a whole. To Venetians, it is quite simply a treasure – one that has immortalized its creator, Baldassare Longhena.

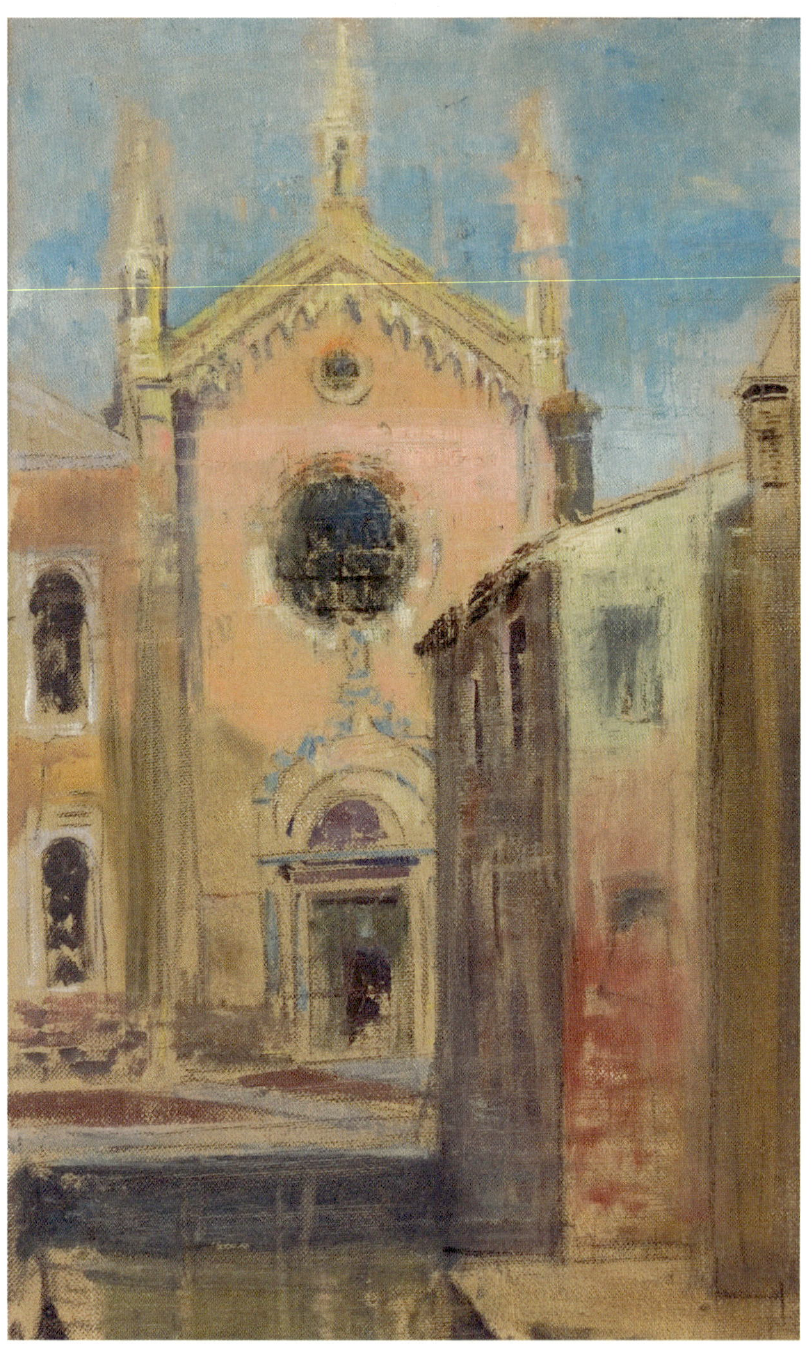

Madonna dell'Orto, *2008*

"[Tiepolo] was buried in the Church of Madonna dell'Orto in the Cannaregio district."

THE RUBENS OF VENICE

Tiepolo was without peer in executing the tricks that make for a believable scene in the heavens . . . Perched so often on scaffolding as he painted, Tiepolo rather naturally developed a fascination for things that hover and fly, flutter and fall.

– Christopher Benfey[39]

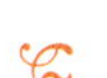

I'm not sure if viewing Venetian masterpieces is supposed to give one a neckache, but anyone who has looked at Giambattista Tiepolo (1696–1770), the eighteenth-century master, knows what I mean. Most of his paintings are high on church ceilings, forcing you to crane your head at oblique angles to see them. The effort is well worth the trouble, however, and you will much sooner recover from this temporary discomfort than from the lingering pleasure of these works. The alternative is much worse: settling for the lifeless reproductions in cheesy guidebooks sold all over Venice, like watching *Citizen Kane* nowadays on an iPod. Tiepolo's murals were meant to be viewed from below, in person, and this is the only way to truly appreciate their dazzling foreshortening and impossible perspective. Horses and chariots dangle from the heavens, and gods and goddesses hover in the clouds. I've observed these paintings for hours (bring a lot of coins for the church's self-service lighting) and am continually humbled by Tiepolo's technical wizardry. His illusionistic, almost hallucinatory "special effects" rival anything Steven Spielberg could create. It is no wonder Tiepolo was idolized like a rock star.

Besides the obvious obstacle of painting upside down, he was forced to re-create entire scenes from his head. Fortunately he was blessed with a prodigious imagination. Sometimes, of course, Tiepolo "cheated" by posing models who resembled the historical figures he painted, such as King Solomon or the Three Wise Men, but this was common artistic practice at the time. During the Renaissance, Michelangelo routinely recruited Arnold Schwarzenegger look-alikes from shipyards to pose for the Sistine Chapel. Tiepolo was immensely resourceful and, like other artists in this great age of painting, he was a thoroughbred, aiming to outpace his peers for the best commissions. The competition was fierce, and success demanded having more than one saleable skill. Knowing how to paint religious subjects was high on the list; even during the Age of Enlightenment, when secular painting was emerging as a market force, artists were in constant demand by the Catholic Church. Tiepolo was no exception, priding himself on his ability to illustrate biblical stories, while drawing inspiration from his contemporaries. When necessary he freely copied, lifting ideas from Veronese, as Veronese had from Titian. "Good artists borrow," as the saying goes, "great artists steal."

I must confess that Tiepolo eluded me at first. Initially I had dismissed his Venetian works as superficial – the kind of decorative painting one finds in an eighteenth-century boudoir. Oddly, it was only after seeing the work of his son Domenico – whom I had mistaken for the father – at Ca' Rezzonico, that I realized what I had been missing. The colors of the frescoes (he learned well from his *paterfamilias*) were vibrant and fresh, a welcome departure from the darker, more somber palette of earlier painters. Of the two, Giambattista, however, is undoubtedly the master. His sheer output rivals Rubens. Like the Flemish artist, his workshop churned out twelve-foot canvases by the dozen.

The son of a sea captain, Tiepolo was by all accounts a prodigy. At fourteen, he studied with the Venetian painter Gregorio Lazzarini, an artist whose skill at rendering large crowds no doubt affected his young apprentice. Tiepolo is often compared with Veronese, but he was influenced more by Giambattista Piazzetta and Sebastiano Ricci. His first mural was commissioned by the Bigliano family, Venetian nobles who made their fortune from book publishing. Over the course of seventy-five years, Tiepolo created nearly a thousand paintings and more than two thousand drawings (good thing he started young). Wielding a genius born not of divine intervention but rather countless hours devoted to his craft (Malcolm Gladwell, in his book *Outliers*, suggests such mastery starts at 10,000 hours[40]), Tiepolo was among the last of the Venetian school, harkening back to a time when a painting could change the world. He straddled the end of the baroque and the beginning of the rococo, and his later works were commissions for the highly ornamented palace of Prince-Bishop Carl-Philipp in Wurzburg, including some of the largest frescoes ever made. They were so immense that Tiepolo had to enlist his sons to help finish them. Parenting has its perks.

I wish I could paint on the scale of Tiepolo, but I've never been able to. I generally work outdoors, and it is a struggle to manage with a canvas larger than what can be carried under my arm. But I do fantasize that someday I'll be able to make a mural-sized landscape, requiring a ladder and scaffold to render unreachable sky and clouds. Monet used long brushes to cover large swaths of his water lily compositions, and the Abstract Expressionist Robert Motherwell had elaborate rolling tracks for his canvases, which spanned the length of his studio. Indeed, there is something appealingly epic about these dimensions.

In 2004, while holding the position of Visiting Artist at the American Academy in Rome, I was assigned a studio in the Stanford White–designed complex, which had ceilings almost thirty feet high. My space was one of four pavilions, originally created for sculptors, that flanked both sides of the main building. They were built at the end of the nineteenth century, at a time when Gilded Age practitioners like Daniel Chester French and Augustus Saint-Gaudens were making casts for the Lincoln Memorial and the original Madison Square Garden. These artists needed enormous height for their larger-than-life works, and though I only needed a table, a stool, and a wall to pin my pictures to, the gargantuan room was not wasted on me; I relished its airy enormity.

Another Venetian muralist was Jacopo Tintoretto, born much earlier, in 1518. Known as *il Furioso*, he was once described by Gore Vidal as the "Cecil B. DeMille of Painting."[41] Vasari, in his *Lives of the Painters*, one of the most enduring books of the Renaissance, writes of this master, "he was swift, resolute, fantastic and extravagant and the most extraordinary brain that the art of painting has ever produced." [42] Tintoretto is best known for the Scuola Grande di San Rocco, in the *sestiere* of San Polo. There he fulfilled the commission of a lifetime, painting no fewer than fifty-two pictures: *The Crucifixion, Adam and Eve, The Visitation, The Adoration of the Magi,* and *The Massacre of the Innocents* being foremost among them. Legend has it that Tintoretto won the commission by forgoing his fee. Posterity, he claimed, was his reward, and today San Rocco is indeed one of the most popular sightseeing destinations in Venice.

For Tiepolo, like Tintoretto, there was a method to rendering murals seemingly as big as a football field. He prepared small studies first, so-called cartoons, which he subsequently transposed onto the wall using an overlay of grids. I have seen some of these preliminary sketches at the Met, and it is clear that these diminutive oils are précis.

Down the hall from these works are two huge panels, *The Triumph of Marius* and *Fall of Verona*, depicting battle scenes from Roman antiquity. They are hung high on the wall, dominating the top of the grand staircase and dwarfing the viewer. Their atmospheric perspective, especially of raging battles in the distance, is the work of a man who could paint the sweep of history as well as Gibbon could write it.

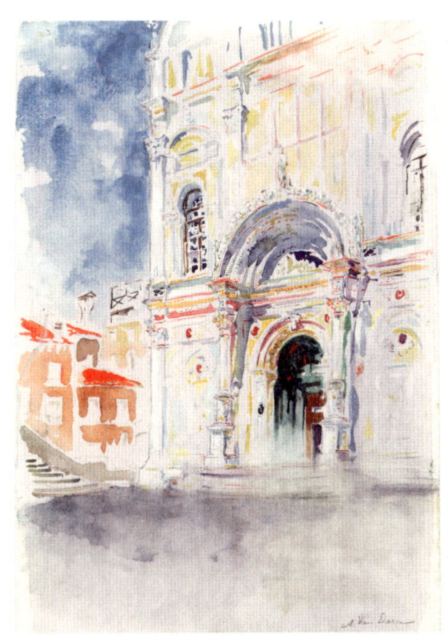

Entry to the Ospedale, *2005*

Tiepolo spent most of his life in Venice, where he was born (he was buried in the Church of Madonna dell'Orto in the Cannaregio district). His travels to Spain and Germany came later in his career; before then, he rarely set foot out of the Veneto. And there was a reason: as a revered artist and native son, Tiepolo was awarded more work than he could possibly handle. His murals adorn the Scoula Grande dei Carmini, the Church of Il Gesuati, and Palazzo Ca' Dolfin. It is illuminating, if not exhausting – given how prolific he was – to travel as I have done from one Tiepolo masterwork to another. I remain especially impressed by how his murals integrate with the surrounding architecture, evoking the far-fetched fantasy of buildings made to accommodate paintings, and not the other way around.

What I find most striking about Tiepolo is his sense of composition: it is storytelling at its best. Characters inhabit his pictures like gifted actors on a stage. The writer Mary McCarthy likened them to rows of figures in a circus, in which everyone's a clown or trapeze artist in theatrical costume.[43] They exude unmistakable emotion, and are rendered with the sensuality and wit of an artist in love with painting. The draftsmanship, particularly of figures, is fluid and assured and exhibits all the signs of rigorous classical training. Take a look at *Institution of the Rosary*, from 1739, and you might walk away feeling that Tiepolo's genius embodies the entire history of Venetian painting all at once. When he died, well into the eighteenth century, it was the end of an era that had begun with Giorgione's languid pastorals of the High Renaissance. The great art historian Bernard Berenson said of him: "Tiepolo is less the end of the era than the beginning of the new . . . The works he left in Spain do more than a little to explain the revival of painting in that country under Goya."[44]

Tiepolo was one of the first masters I started copying. While I was in graduate school in architecture, I took a leave of absence to take art courses at the National Academy in New York, studying both watercolor and life drawing. On the days between classes, when I had time to myself, I went to the museums, studying firsthand the works of Delacroix, Vermeer, Raeburn, Millet, Degas, Manet – and Tiepolo. It was a self-imposed education, one I fashioned after the examples I'd read in my copy of *The Penguin Dictionary of Artists*, a collection of artists' biographies from Giotto to Van Gogh. I was taken with how, with few exceptions, each artist had followed the same career path: precocious at a young age (usually fourteen or fifteen), they were discovered by local artists, who later invited them to be apprentices in their workshops. There the impressionable youths were taught to duplicate their master's style, learning it sufficiently to assist on larger paintings and to eventually go out on their own. It was a winning formula. In my case, however, it was too late to be precocious, though I had, in fact, been drawing from an early age; and I knew I was not going to be an apprentice (somehow that practice died out with the eighteenth century). But at least I could copy. The Met, Frick,

Whitney, Guggenheim, and Morgan all had policies that encouraged this practice, though only pencil was allowed, not paints.

I spent most of my time at the Met, since it is only a block from my apartment, and it was there I first became acquainted with Tiepolo. In retrospect, his large murals now seem very different from the ones I later saw in Venice, which are much more delicate and flowery. The figures in them seemed bigger and more imposing; in hindsight, however, they were hung much closer to eye level than the frescos in Venice, which were forty feet above me – and the simple fact that they are life-size made them easier to draw. I studied up close the skillful modeling of the muscular arms and legs, and took note of the complex poses. Tiepolo's understanding of anatomy was remarkable. Over the course of several days, I made numerous studies of faces, necks, and torsos. I singled out individual figures from the crowd scenes that I wanted to render and made detailed sketches of them. It was a relief to draw people who were perfectly still, rather than the models in school who couldn't sustain a pose without shifting or falling asleep.

Tiepolo made me hungry to copy more paintings by different artists, and I moved on to other galleries in the museum, such as the American Wing, where the Sargents, Homers, and Stuarts are hung. From a painting by Thomas Eakins, entitled *Mrs. Mary Arthur,* of an old woman knitting a sweater, I made a careful study of each bony finger of her tightly held grip. From a painting by Sargent, of "Madame X," I learned how powerful a profile can be. Drawing the human figure was different from drawing buildings, but I found common ground in each. There is an architecture to both, and though I instinctively knew this, it was through my own observation with pencil in hand that I came to truly understand it.

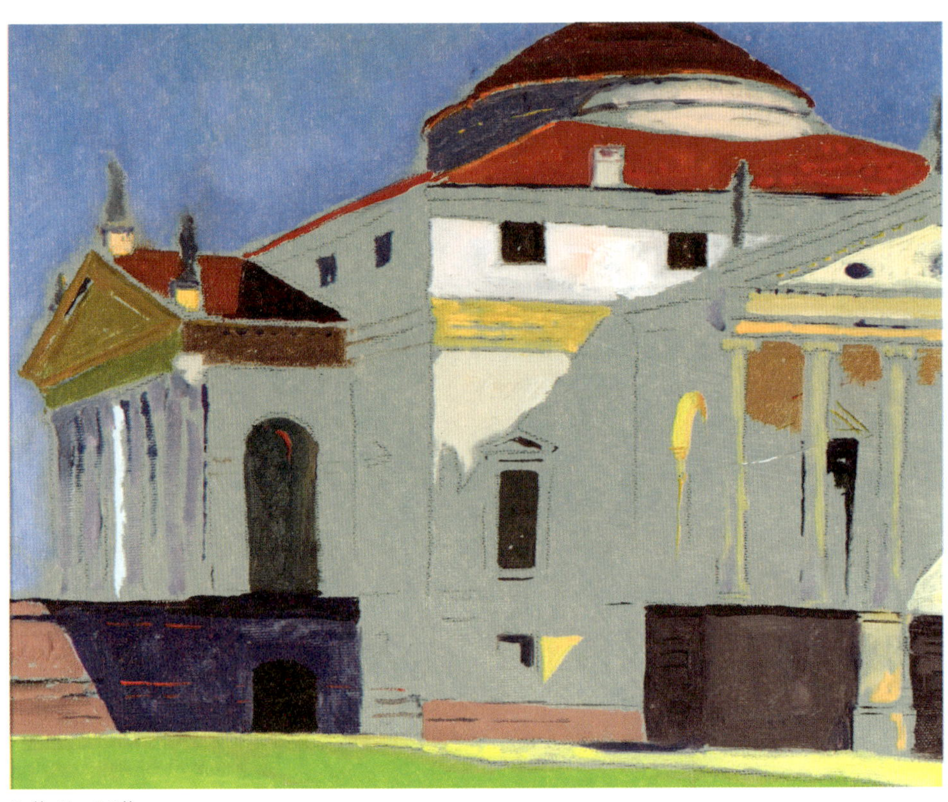

Palladian Villa, *2010*

"Palladio not only redefined how country villas . . . were designed but also redefined their meaning."

IN SEARCH OF PALLADIO

Venice was enveloped for centuries in the spell cast by Palladio's architecture.

– James Ackerman [45]

The greatest architect in Venice's long history, Andrea Palladio, was not born there, but in the neighboring city of Padua, and most of his buildings are in nearby Vicenza. Yet his three most famous churches – the Redentore, San Giorgio, and San Zitelle – are happily ensconced in La Serenissima. They form a distinctive trio along one stretch of the lagoon, all within a mile of one another and comprise some of the finest examples of Renaissance architecture in Europe. If Palladio, originally apprenticed as a stonemason, had designed nothing else in his life, his name would be secure with any one of these landmarks. Any architect would dream for such recognition. As the celebrated modernist architect I. M. Pei once said of his own work, "I would gladly trade it all for just one of Louis Kahn's masterpieces."[46]

Palladio is known not only for his churches, but for his villas as well. They are the subject of countless books and are considered precursors to modernist architecture. Maser, Barbaro, "La Malcontenta," "La Rotonda": these are the mansions that line the banks of the River

Brenta outside Venice, like châteaux on the Loire. They are reminders of the Venetian gentry who once lived there – the Veneto being a sort of Hamptons of its day – that offered an escape from the heat of a city that could be suffocating in the summer. One doesn't even want to imagine how the Grand Canal smelled in August.

My first tour of these villas came in the summer of 1985 when I was invited by Regina Resnik, the aforementioned family friend, on a ride through the countryside. We drove on back roads, packed tightly in her little Fiat. She steered valiantly through ruts and dirt. Our open window was the only air-conditioning as we passed allées of cypress trees and small farm stands. Quaint towns came and went, many before we had a chance to catch their names; each had a square, a church, a small trattoria, a statue of the Virgin Mary, and of course a *gelateria*. On the outskirts, vineyards dotted the low hillsides, beckoning us to stop and sample their vintages.

Our first destination was Villa Barbaro. An inclined walkway, which we could see through iron gates, led to the entrance. The temple front had Ionic pilasters and bright yellow stucco on the façade. Pristine green lawn bordered both sides of the front court, and huge sundials, inscribed on the face of two flanking wings, were prominently displayed, symbols of the husbandry they once glorified. We pried ourselves out of the car, and entered the grounds. I can hardly think of a better guide to these palaces than Regina, who has spent her life on the stage. As we strolled the corridors, I could almost imagine her singing a solo from Puccini, commensurate with the setting. It called to mind the 1979 film version of *Don Giovanni*, directed by Joseph Losey, one of the most stirring interpretations of an opera I've ever seen, in which every scene takes place in a Palladian villa. These mansions were the ultimate backdrop for Don Juan's amorous conquests. Ironically, La Rotonda was originally commissioned in 1565 by the presumably celibate Paolo Almerico, a priest who held a high rank with the Vatican.

The layout of the rooms at Villa Barbaro is beautifully choreographed, for Palladio clearly had a sense of the ceremonial. The spaces glide from one to the next like an aria, and the doorways are aligned in perfect succession like a hall of mirrors. Elaborate frescoes by Veronese, the sixteenth-century painter also known as Paolo Caliari, adorn the walls, and his *trompe l'œil* murals are part architectural fantasy, part costume party. They seamlessly integrate with the interior architecture, enveloping each room in the most beautiful wall covering ever made. Leaving Regina to herself for a moment, I wandered alone through the house. I felt I was being watched, and, indeed, elegant dukes and duchesses, creations of Veronese's hand, peered from all corners of the room, inviting me to bow before them. My curiosity led me outside, and passing through a series of french doors, I found a gravel path with folding green chairs – the kind I always associate with the Luxembourg Gardens in Paris. Taking a seat, I contemplated the façade. The symmetry was subtle and understated; Palladio was not advertising his ego the way some celebrity architects do. This was not classicism on steroids, but at its lean and sinewy best.

Andrea Palladio, originally named Andrea di Pietro della Gondola, was born in 1508, the son of a miller. He was mentored as a young man by the humanist Count Gian Giorgio Trissino, who came from Vicenza, and who later gave him the name Palladio, after Pallas Athene, the Greek goddess of wisdom. Commissions followed, from Venetian patrons such as the Barbaro, Correr, Pisani, and Foscari families, and Palladio's statue grew such that he was considered for the prestigious position of Proto della Serenissima, or Chief Architect of Venice, though he did not ultimately get it. Two years ago I saw an exhibit of his architectural drawings at the Morgan Library in New York, which displayed the elegance of his style and his deep reverence for historical precedent. It is interesting to note how this

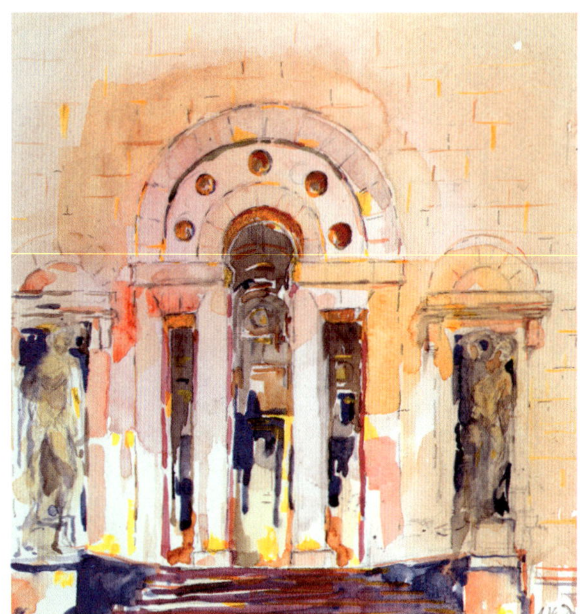

Villa Poiana, *1988*

great figure – a tireless student of those before him – has become the most copied architect in the world.

Palladio's influence on later architects was enormous. One of his greatest followers was Thomas Jefferson. Monticello, in Charlottesville, Virginia, is an homage to the Italian master. Featured on the back of the nickel, Jefferson's great house was designed and built over the course of forty years, which nearly bankrupted the third president. Its side wings gracefully balance the composition and naturally embrace the surrounding grounds. There are distinct references to the local vernacular – the use of Virginia brick especially – which Palladio would have applauded. White Tuscan columns at the front and rear evoke a sense of grandeur. For Jefferson, Palladio's classical references were more than aesthetically pleasing; they reflected the ideals of the Roman Republic, a source very dear to the founding fathers. In 1989 I was given a tour of the octagonal dome (a late improvement by Jefferson) by a professor at the University of Virginia, the campus of which Jefferson also designed. I was struck by how modest the room is: there was no furniture to speak of, and the floors are composed of simple wood planks.

Palladio not only redefined how country villas such as Jefferson's were designed, but also redefined their meaning and purpose. Indeed "Palladianism" is a term used by scholars to describe architecture that aspires to his style. Elevating the gentleman's farmhouse to a stately building type, Palladio, as a humanist at the height of the Renaissance, saw man – not God – as the touchstone for his proportions (akin to Leonardo's famous drawing of a male figure outstretched in a circle). Heavily influenced by Vitruvius – whose volume *The Ten Books on Architecture* (60 A.D.) notes that "nature has designed the human body so that its members can be duly proportional to the frame as a whole"[47] – Palladio's Villa Rotonda, designed in 1565, is the quintessential example of this ideal. The relationships between column and capital, and cornice and frieze, derive from similar ratios in the human form, and the four exterior façades or "faces" of La Rotonda are identical, each portico being oriented to face the 360-degree views of the hills beyond. (Witold Rybczynski, however, one of my favorite writers on architecture, wonders whether these matching elevations more resemble a four-headed monster than a human being.[48]) The building's plan is essentially the intersection of a square and a cross, and even though the villa has a dome – one of only a few Palladio ever planned for a house – it is not ostentatious, and was most probably the model for Monticello.

As an undergraduate, I was assigned to make a one-quarter-scale model of a Palladian structure. Though fellow students were incredulous, I embraced the concept, and with some trepidation, chose La Rotonda as my building. The exercise was the brainchild of our Columbia professor Robert A. M. Stern, at that time one of the leading proponents of the postmodernist movement. Stern, now dean of Yale's School of Architecture, relished inculcating us with this task – try using an X-Acto knife to make a dome out of foam core – because he believed the exercise would metamorphose us into budding classicists. His final words of "encouragement," delivered with a impish smile, were: "For God's sake, don't cut yourself and get blood on the model!" Thankfully, I managed to finish without going to the emergency room. And, though I was exhausted from lack of sleep, I had acquired a new appreciation of Palladio's genius. No matter how I held the model – upside down, sideways, or from above – it always looked symmetrical. Stern beamed. He had catechized yet another anchorite for his new École des Beaux-Arts in Morningside Heights. Later, when I presented my rendering of the building in watercolor, in the style of a nineteenth-century atelier, I saw how the plans, section, and elevations could be beautiful works of art in themselves.

Ultimately, the legacy of Palladio, for me, is that he is a joy to paint. His forms are so pure and simple, so devoid of superfluous ornamentation, that it takes little effort to get them right. His architecture can be deceptive – it took me a while to realize this, and if you neglect the larger mass for the smaller details, you will not see the structure for the abstraction it is. With the Redentore, for example, I first block in the volumes as solid shapes of color, carefully filling them to their outside edges, like painting by number. Then I add a few accents of shade and shadow to soften the forms. When I'm done, the picture seems more "true" than if I'd painstakingly included every single pediment, pilaster, and entablature.

One perception of Palladio's architecture is that it is cold and detached. But what did his contemporaries think of his work? Some experts conjecture he was considered radical, revolutionary, even eccentric. His buildings were a dramatic shift from the preceding Gothic, and his monumentalism might well have intimidated the Venetians of his day. I've come to see Palladio as an artist of the first order who created an aesthetic that, however rooted in ancient history, was entirely personal and relevant, the product of a rational yet not

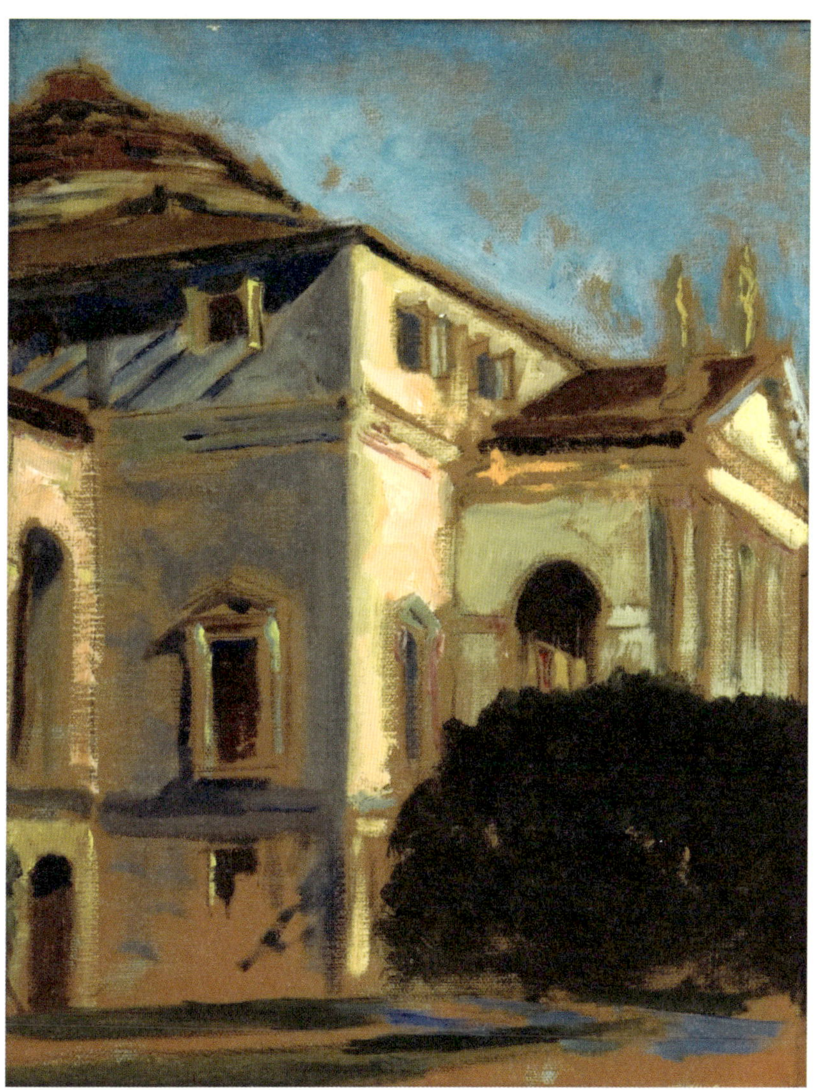

Villa Rotonda, *2008*

dispassionate mind. In 1986 I made a pilgrimage to Vicenza, fifty miles west of Venice, to seek some answers and clarify my opinion. The small city is a grand gallery of Palladio's architecture, and the Chamber of Commerce will not let you forget it: there is a Palladio hotel, a Palladio café, a Palladio gift shop, and a Palladio statue in the center of town. I was accompanied by a friend from college, Matt Viederman, now a practicing architect in New York, and we both came armed with sketchbooks. Taking James Ackerman's volume of essays, *Palladio: Architect and Society* (which our professor, Eugene Santomosso, had recommended), we mapped out the dimensions of buildings such as the Teatro Olimpicio, the Palazzo Chiericati, and the Palazzo Thiene. I snapped a picture of Matt standing at the base of one of the columns, and confirmed how his proportions resembled, on a smaller scale, the building's own. Looking at a balustrade, each baluster was divided into three sections, with a "head," "torso," and "feet": it was the same anthropomorphic relationship we'd studied in the early skyscrapers of Louis Sullivan, such as the Wainwright building in St. Louis – an 1890 brick building with a top, middle, and bottom, so to speak, comprising a massive cornice, a distinct middle section, and a heavy base.

Palladio's legacy is not limited to the buildings he designed. He also wrote a famous treatise on architecture: *I Quattro Libri*, or *Four Books of Architecture*. It was published in Venice by Franceschi, and is more than 340 pages long. It includes his woodcut illustrations of bridges, churches, and diagrams of the five orders, some of which he distilled from earlier important treastises of Serlio and Vitruvius. The books traveled far, becoming the standard text for aspiring architects for three hundred years, and prompted Jefferson to write in a letter to a friend: "Palladio is the Bible, stick close to it."[49] Though not intended to be scholarly, or even philosophical, they have become part of the pantheon. As recently as the 1980s there was a revival of interest in the *Four Books,* and several new editions were printed. It became for a time the so-called manifesto for the postmodernists, whose leaders besides Stern include Robert Venturi, Michael Graves, Thomas Beeby, and Philip Johnson, the designer of the famous Glass House. These architects recognized that Palladio was one of the first to emphasize the importance of the plan as the generating component of any design, the same message Frank Lloyd Wright would preach centuries later. Decoration was significant to Palladio, especially in his use of statuary, but he did not believe it should necessarily dominate the composition. "Form follows function" might well have been his own adage had he spoken English, and one could argue that aspects of Mies van der Rohe's designs were influenced by Palladio, even if the German, famous for the Seagram Building in New York, may not have chosen to acknowledge it.

Palladio, in a word, got it. Like every architect during the Renaissance, he was inspired by ancient ruins. But he did not merely imitate; he refined them until they became relevant, and his own. This is no meager accomplishment. In the end, it is not just about geometry, but, as Rybczynski points out in his book on Palladio, *The Perfect House*, the more elusive and intangible *harmony*.[50] If you don't have an instinct for it, it is hard to codify or teach it. "Architecture is a 'dumb' art," Stern once told us. "Keep it simple. Don't try to make it more complicated than it already is." It is this maxim to which I've aspired in all my Venetian paintings.

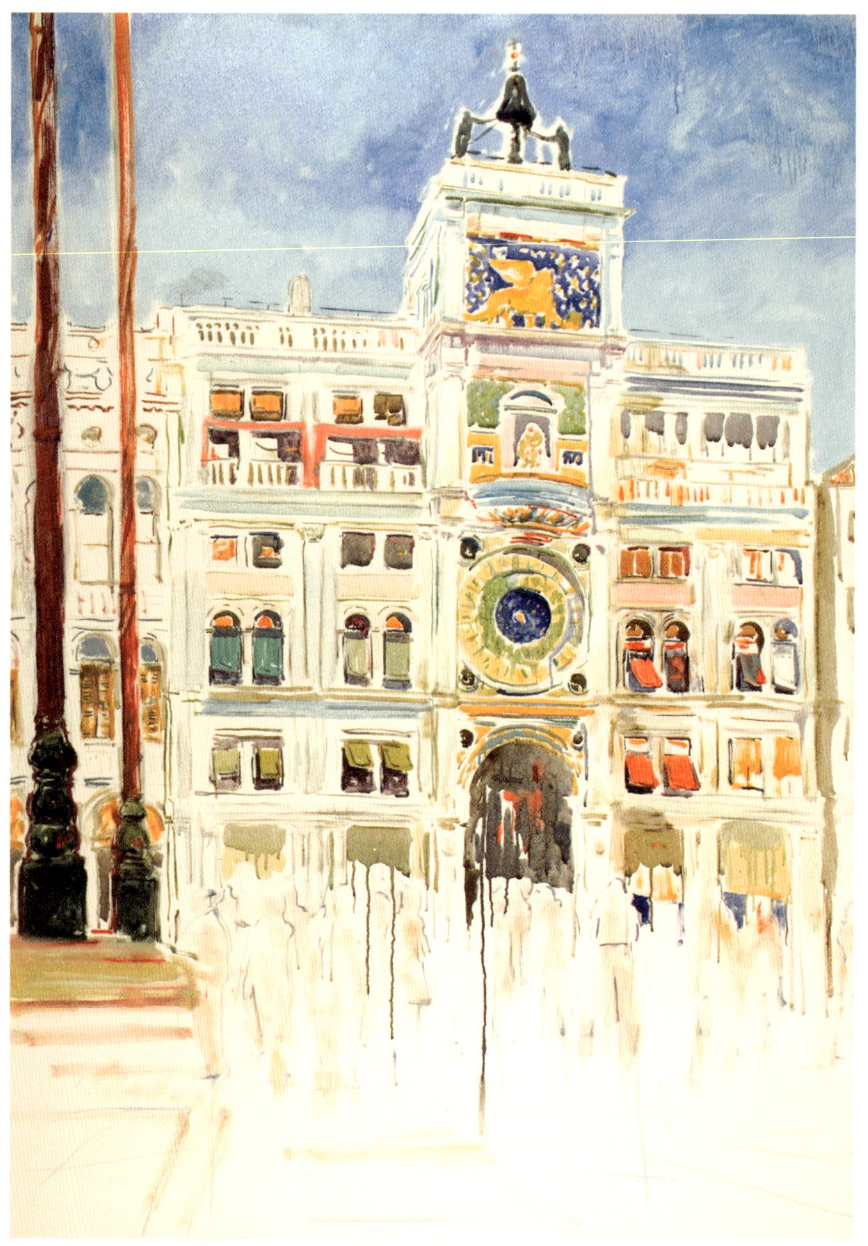

The Clocktower, *2010*

"It was hard for me to explain exactly why, but there was something in my recent Venetian pictures that was markedly different."

AFTERWORD

To build a city where it is impossible . . .
is madness in itself, but to build one
of the grandest of cities is the
madness of genius.

– Alexander Herzen [51]

It was the fall of 2010, and I had just finished hanging my paintings for an upcoming exhibit at 130 West Fifty-Seventh Street in New York. The space, which I also maintain as a studio, is a large loft with double-height windows and a six-foot fireplace. For many years, the artist Charles Baskerville, a noted portrait painter, occupied the atelier after inheriting it from Childe Hassam, who lived there from 1908 to 1930. Two large skylights, located high on the ceiling, let in the last of the day's light. As I surveyed the scene from an interior balcony, I tried to imagine I was merely an objective viewer, not the artist whose works were on display. It was difficult to do. All I could see were the flaws in my pictures, the missteps of color and composition. Self-doubt started to creep in, the feeling I get whenever I sift through old canvases at flea markets, wondering whether I will be one of those same discarded artists. I wanted to grab a paintbrush and start over. I wished I could postpone the show altogether. But the opening was in an hour, and I resigned myself.

Turning away from my paintings, I looked out the window, to a prewar building across the street. The Gothic-style structure, eighteen stories high and built above a Baptist church, reminded me of the Ca' d'Oro in Venice. Stone figures of saints, set in niches, were sculpted across the top of the parapet. They gazed back at me solemnly, like inscrutable art critics. Were they judging me? Were they out to get me? A little pregame paranoia got the best of me. Returning my attention to the gallery, I took another look at my work and I couldn't help but notice how many of my paintings were of Venice. Like the serene collections of bottles in still life painter Giorgio Morandi's work, my scenes of the city were often of the same building, simply rendered from different angles. It wasn't my intention for the show to be so one-sided, but these were the pictures I liked the most. I couldn't help but feel partial to the images of the Dogana, Giudecca, and the Salute over the other works on display depicting Paris, Rome, London, and New York. For they reminded me of the place where I had first decided to become a painter.

It was hard for me to explain exactly why, but there was something in my recent Venetian pictures that was markedly different: they seemed less detailed, less cautious. The subject matter, as usual, was buildings, but these works less and less resembled architectural renderings; at last they looked like *paintings*. Most of them had been done *in situ*, while a few, out of necessity, were done in the studio, transposed onto canvas from sketches in my notebooks. *Plein air* painting, for all its virtues, has its limitations: it requires moderate weather, and during the winter I avoid working in the cold. Whistler solved the problem by working from memory, a trick he learned from his Beaux-Arts training: his professors taught him how to observe nature so intensely he could memorize what he saw and visualize it later in his studio.

My style, consciously or unconsciously, reflects the artists of Venice I admired. With Arbit Blatas in mind, I blur the perspective of certain night scenes. From Walter Sickert, I've reduced my palette and added darker grounds. From Turner, I render waves of the sea with more volume. But beyond the influence of these masters, my own experience of living in Venice has ultimately shaped the way I paint. I've become a devoted student of its history and its art – its "anatomy" if you will – and a keen observer of its ever-changing physiognomy. This frame of reference informs my perception and work. When I've drawn portraits of people, I've come to prefer drawing someone I know, rather than an anonymous model. Otherwise, his or her face has little meaning to me, and it becomes harder to bring to life. In the end, I now suppose, it is less about *what* I see than *how* I see it.

As the guests began to arrive, I was apprehensive. How would the show be received? Would they notice my jitters? Whatever reassurance I mustered came from the lesson of Venice itself: almost by definition, it is a city borne out of creative optimism – a world on water that shouldn't have been. But its mere existence is in the end an inspiration, a call to be less predictable, more buoyant. As my artist friend (and fellow Venetophile) David Levine once said about painting: "It is simple. You must learn how to play."

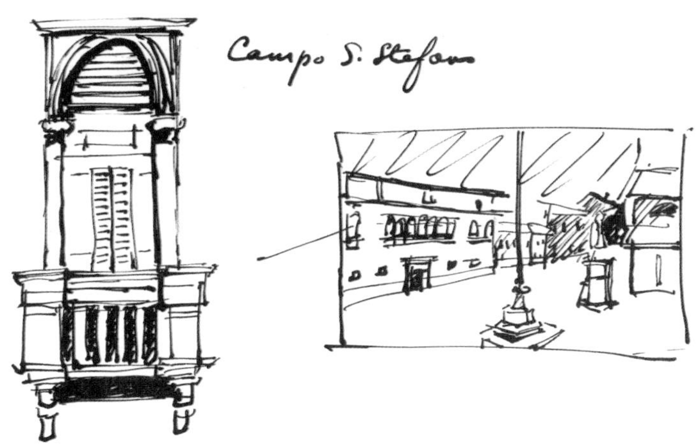

Window with Balcony, *1986*

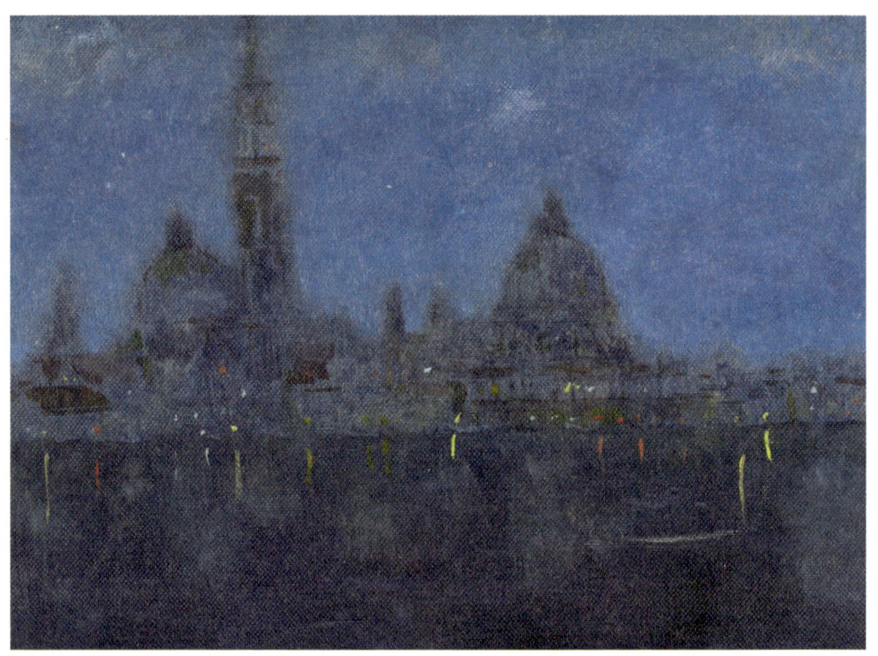

Venice at Night, *2008*

GLOSSARY

THE ACCADEMIA · The Gallerie dell'Accademia is Venice's most famous art gallery, and it houses important pre-nineteenth-century paintings. It was originally founded as an art academy in 1750. Among the many masters in its collection are Carpaccio, Bellotto, Mantegna, and Vasari. In 1573, Paolo Veronese unveiled the gallery's largest painting, *The Feast in the House of Levi,* which is more than forty-two feet long. After a two-year restoration the gallery has reopened in 2011.

RICHARD PARKES BONINGTON · An extraordinarily precocious artist, Bonington died before he was thirty, but by the age of twenty-four he had already become one of the most influential British artists of his time. Particularly skilled in watercolor, he won many contemporary admirers, including none other than Delacroix, who considered him a genius. Bonington made many studies of Venice, including those of the Campo San Giovanni e Paolo, the Doge's Palace, and Piazza San Marco.

CARNIVAL · This elaborate costume celebration is an annual event in Venice that supposedly began in 1162 to commemorate an important victory over Ulrico. Carnival originally commenced on the first day after Christmas and was popular until the 1700s. It has since been revived and now takes place for two weeks before Ash Wednesday and ends on Shrove Tuesday. The festival attracts upwards of 30,000 people. The masks that participants wear for the occasion are sold all over the city and are often exquisitely made.

CUSTOMS HOUSE · Known as the Dogana di Mare, this sixteenth-century structure has a bittersweet history. Only decades after the Dogana was built, Venice's trading empire began to decline rapidly and eventually the city was bankrupt. The Dogana was built as a symbol of Venice's commercial power, and was erected to allow custom officials to inspect incoming cargo ships. The current building, a replacement of an older fourteenth-century edifice, is crowned by two Atlas figures holding a bronze globe. A statue of Fortuna rises at its apex. Henry James wrote in *The Italian Hours*: "This Fortuna . . . catches the wind in the bit of drapery of which she has divested her rotary bronze loveliness."[52]

DORSODURO • One of the six *sestieri*, or districts of Venice, "Dorsoduro" translates in Italian as "high ridge" (it has a slightly higher elevation than the rest of the city). It is surrounded by St. Mark's Basin and both the Giudecca and the Grand Canal, and is decidedly less touristy than other neighborhoods in Venice. As the Accademia and the Peggy Guggenheim Museum are located on this peninsula, there is a tradition of artists and writers living here.

THE FENICE • Teatro la Fenice, Venice's heavily ornate baroque opera house, was first built in 1774, and has been heavily damaged by fires at least three times. Since then it has been entirely rebuilt, including most recently in 1996, after a disgruntled contractor intentionally set it ablaze. Verdi's *Rigoletto* and *La Traviata* premiered there in the nineteenth century. Though quite small compared with other European opera houses, its intimacy adds to its charm.

CAFFÈ FLORIAN • One of the oldest continously running coffeehouses in Europe (it was founded in 1720), the lavishly decorated Florian is located in Piazzo San Marco, just below the Campanile. Carlo Goldoni was one of its earliest customers, and Casanova was known to have frequented it, since it was the only café to admit women at the time. Other patrons included Proust, Lord Bryon, Modigliani, and Stravinsky.

CAMPO SANTA MARIA FORMOSA • This large Venetian square in the Sestiere di Castello is named for the church of the same name at the sourthern end of the *campo*, which was designed in 1492 by Mauro Codussi. The elegant Hotel Scandinavia is included among the buildings in the *campo*, and it occupies a palace that was built on a foundation that is nearly 1,000 years old. A noteworthy bell tower, built next to the church, was completed in 1688.

THE GHETTO • Though Jews lived in Venice for centuries, for many years they were restricted to a specific *sestiere,* the Cannaregio district, where they had to maintain evening curfews. Often overcrowded, this area, divided into the Ghetto Nuovo (New Ghetto) and Ghetto Vecchio (Old Ghetto), has the tallest residential buildings in Venice, some as high as seven stories. As lenders, the Jews were particularly useful to the wealthy Venetian state.

GIUDECCA • The Giudecca is an oblong island which lies opposite the Venetian Lagoon from the Zattere, and was once known as Spinalongas ("long spur") because of its shape. Over time, its noble families abandoned this location because shipyards and more industrialized areas were encroaching. Now the island has returned to being a fashionable residential area. The Redentore church by Palladio is perhaps its most recognizable landmark. The Convertiti convent, a female prison, is also located here.

FRANCESCO GUARDI • Like Canaletto, Guardi (born in 1712) was known for his scenes, or *veduti,* of Venice. His style, however, is much more modern than Canaletto, with looser brush strokes, and less exacting detail. His brothers Niccolò and Gian Antonio were also prominent painters. Some of his more well-known works include twelve pictures, entitled *The Doge's Feasts,* which he completed in 1763 for the Doge Alvise Mocenigo. Besides Canaletto, Guardi was influenced by the painter Luca Carlevarijs.

LOCANDA MONTIN • A famous restaurant in Venice's Dorsoduro district, the Montin is known for its outdoor garden which has an elaborate trellis and vines. Ezra Pound and Modigliani were frequent guests, as was President Jimmy Carter, who came in the 1980s. More recently, Robert De Niro, Yoko Ono, Brad Pitt, and Mick Jagger have been guests. Arbit Blatas painted a picture of it in 1971.

MARINO MARINI • Born in 1901 in Postoia, Marini was famous for his equestrian statues. He was influenced by the sculptor Artur Martini and later became friends with Giacometti during visits to Basel. In 1950, the Bucholz Gallery in New York began exhibiting his work, and there is now a museum in Florence dedicated to its display. He is also known as a painter and graphic artist, and in 1952 won the first prize at the Biennale exhibit.

JAN MORRIS • Born in 1926 in Somerset, England, the historian and travel writer Jan Morris has written extensively on Venice, and published *Venice* (1960), *The Venetian Empire* (1980), and *A Venetian Bestiary* (1982), among her many works. Oxford, New York City, Trieste, and Hong Kong have also been her subjects. Born James Morris, she underwent a sex change in 1976, which she described in her memoir *Conundrum.*

MAURICE PRENDERGAST • A post-impressionist of the first rank, Prendergast lived in Canada and Boston, and studied in Paris, where he met Whistler and Sickert. Known for his careful watercolor renditions of Venetian cityscapes, he often painted rain scenes with lustrously colored crowds of people donning umbrellas. The Adelson Gallery in New York City has an especially impressive collection of his works. He was a member of the Eight, a group of painters that included Robert Henri, Everett Shinn, and William Glackens.

RIALTO • One of only four bridges to span the Grand Canal, the Rialto has long been a landmark of Venice. Originally it was made of wood, but it was rebuilt in stone in 1591 by Antonio da Ponte. Today, various shops, choked with tacky tourist gifts, flank both sides of its interior. Nevertheless the bridge continues to be a handsome piece of architecture.

SEBASTIANO RICCI • A painter of the Venetian School who flourished in the baroque period, Ricci was born in 1659 and was first apprenticed to Frederico Cerebri. Known for his scandalous affairs (one almost had him executed), he fled Venice more than once, but returned often to complete many commissions, including the *Madonna with Child* for San Giorgio Maggiore. In his last years, he collaborated with his nephew Marco Ricci on several paintings. In addition to Venice, he is known for his work in Parma, Milan, and Rome. He also worked in Paris, where he met Watteau.

JACOPO SANSOVINO • One of Venice's most heralded architects, this Renaissance master was born in 1486 and is perhaps best known for his Biblioteca Marciana, which is located just across from the Palazzo Ducale, and took fifty years to build. Another work of his, also near the palace, is the Loggetta at the base of the Campanile of San Marco. His name was originally Jacopo Tatti, but he changed it in honor of the first architect he apprenticed with, Andrea Sansovino.

SAN GIACOMO DI RIALTO • This ancient church's origins began in the fifth century, when it was first established on the site. The present eleventh-century building, erected near the Rialto market, has an inscription on the cross on the outside apse that proclaims honesty in merchants, the accuracy of weights, and the legality of contracts. The church has survived a major fire and was restored in 1601 by the doge Marino Grimaldi, who made sure that the floors were raised to avoid the chronic flooding during *aqua alta.*

SAN GIORGIO • This is an island in Venice, not far from Piazza San Marco, which is known for its monastery (founded in 982) and a church designed by Palladio in 1566. The Benedictine monk Giovanni Morosini is reputed to have convinced the doge to donate the entire island to the monastery. The island was originally called Insula Memmia because of the Memmo family who owned it.

CARLO SCARPA • The iconoclastic Italian architect, born in 1906 in Venice, lived in Vicenza as a young adult. Heavily influenced by Frank Lloyd Wright and Josef Hoffmann, he began his career as an industrial designer, and throughout his professional life maintained a rigorous sense of detail in his work. He paid great attention to materials, at one point even designing a glass project for the Venini Glassworks. Among his protégés is the internationally known architect Mario Botta.

SCUOLA GRANDE DI SAN ROCCO • Named for St. Roch, a protector against plague, this Scuola was founded in 1478 and stands next to a church which shares its name. Scuolas were organizations – known less as schools than as confraternities – founded on spiritual principles. Tintoretto painted his famous murals here in 1564, and Canaletto created an excellent view of its façade in 1735, showing the pope at its entrance.

WALTER SICKERT • A nineteenth-century Impressionist who was a friend of both Degas and Whistler, Sickert is often referred to as the godfather of British modern art. His fascination with Venice, which he called "the loveliest city in the world," prompted him to submit his painting of Santa Maria della Salute to the Royal Academy upon his election in 1934. Sickert also painted the underbelly of London, depicting cabaret and brothel life.

STUCKY FLOUR MILL • This Victorian structure on the Giudecca is among the tallest in Venice, almost fourteen stories high. The mill was founded by Giovanni Stucky, who sought its location by the water's edge so that his milled flour could easily be shipped by sea. Over time, it also became the site of where Venice's *vaporetti*, or water buses, were manufactured.

VAPORETTO • In 1881 the *vaporetto*, or water bus, first started to offer regular transportation service. In addition to the Grand Canal, they provide access to nearby islands like Murano, Torcello, and Burano. Once steam powered, they are operated by the ACTV (Venetian Public Transportation System). Shaped like small ferries, they run on a twenty-four-hour schedule. Though these boats often seem cumbersome, they offer the most efficient form of travel in the city.

GIORGIO VASARI • In his day, Giorgio Vasari (1511–1574) was a celebrated architect, painter, and writer – the epitome of the Renaissance man. Though his frescoes are largely forgotten, he designed several important buildings, including the Uffizi in Florence. His most lasting achievement was his monumental, somewhat anecdotal, book *The Lives of the Artists,* which is still in print some 500 years after it was first published. This classic work contains short profiles of a great number of artists – from Cimabue and Giotto to Brunelleschi and Bronzino – with particular emphasis on the Florentine masters. An early apprentice of Michelangelo, Vasari is thought to be the first to coin the term "Renaissance."

THE ZATTERE • First built in 1519 as a landing dock for timber for building ships (hence the term *zattere,* for wooden raft), the Zattere has since become a peaceful promenade that offers a welcome respite from the more crowded streets in the city. The baroque church Il Gesuati, designed by Giorgio Massari, is situated here, as is Santa Maria della Visitazione, which is adorned with paintings of fifty-eight saints. At the Zattere's eastern tip is the famed Customs House with its prominent bronze weathervane.

NOTES

1. Fran Lebowitz, quoted in Jennifer Wright, "The Visible City of Venice" (http://www.literarytraveler.com/articles/venice.aspx).
2. Percy Bysshe Shelley, "Julian and Maddalo: A Conversation." *Ode to the West Wind and Other Poems* (Dover Publications, New York, 1993), p. 19.
3. Sir Kenneth Clark, *Civilization,* PBS television series, 1969.
4. John Ruskin, *The Stones of Venice,* ed. Jan Morris (Little, Brown and Company, Boston, 1981), p. 29.
5. Thomas Okey, *The Old Venetian Palaces and Old Venetian Folk* (E. P. Dutton and Co., New York, 1908), p. 174.
6. Hugh Honour, *The Companion Guide to Venice* (St. Edmondsbury Press, Ltd., Suffolk, 1996), p. 23.
7. Wolfgang Kemp, *The Desire of My Eyes: The Life and Work of John Ruskin* (Farrar Straus and Giroux, New York, 1990), p. 156.
8. Van Akin Bard, *Christmas Story: John Ruskin's Venetian Letters of 1876–77* (Associated University Presses, London, 1990), p. 36.
9. Jan Morris, ed., *John Ruskin: The Stones of Venice* (Little, Brown and Company, Boston, 1981), p. 36.
10. Hippolyte Taine, *Italy: Florence and Venice* (Henry Holt, New York, 1889), p. 38.
11. Morris, ed., *John Ruskin: The Stones of Venice*, p. 37.
12. Deborah Howard, *The Architectural History of Venice* (Yale University Press, New Haven, CT, 2002) p. 194.
13. John Updike (interview with Adam Van Doren, Beverly Farms, MA, July 1994).
14. Margaret McDonald, *Palaces in the Night: Whistler in Venice* (University of California Press, 2001), p. 32.
15. Robin Spence, ed., *Whistler: A Retrospective* (Wings Books, New York, 1989), p. 46.
16. Arbit Blatas, *An Artist's Venice* (Vendome Press, New York, 1997), p. 52.
17. Ralph Blumenthal, "Arbit Blatas, 90, A Sculptor, Painter and Stage Designer," *The New York Times*, April 28, 1999.
18. John Esten, *Sargent Painting Out-of-Doors* (Universe Publishing, New York, 2000), p. 66.
19. Michael Kimmelman, *The New York Times* (Arts and Leisure section, March 2003).

20. Willliam Wordsworth, *Selected Poetry of William Wordsworth*, ed. Mark Van Doren (Modern Library, New York, 2002), p. 64.
21. Julian Halsby, *Venice: The Artist's Vision* (Unicorn Press, London, 1990), p. 17.
22. Ian Chilvers, *Oxford Dictionary of Art* (Oxford University Press, London, 1988), p. 99.
23. Byron Dobell, "For David Levine" (*Southampton Review,* Vol. IV, no. 1, Stony Brook, Spring 2010), p. 143.
24. Mark Van Doren, *A Country Year* (Henry Holt, New York, 1939), p. 71.
25. Charles Dickens, *Pictures fom Italy* (Harper and Brothers, New York, 1877), p. 39.
26. Dorothea Ritter, *Venice in Old Photographs,* John Julius Norwich, intro. (Little, Brown and Company, Boston, 1994), p. 18.
27. Honour, *The Companion Guide to Venice*, p. 17.
28. Thomas Gray, "The Presbyterian Magazine," vol. 2; C. Van Rensselear, ed. (Wm H. Mitchell Publishers, Philadelphia, 1852), p. 372.
29. Morris, ed., *John Ruskin: The Stones of Venice*, p. 43.
30. Henry James, *Collected Travel Writings* (Library of America, New York, 1993), p. 295.
31. Mark Twain, *A Tramp Abroad* (American Publishng Company, Hartford, CT, 1908), p. 255.
32. Lord Byron, *Childe Harold's Pilgrimage* [I Stood in Venice] (Biblio Bazaar, 2006), p. 78.
33. Howard, *The Architectural History of Venice*, p. 78.
34. Jan Morris, *A Venetian Bestiary* (Faber & Faber, New York, 2007).
35. Theodore K. Rabb, "Titian, Tintoretto and Veronese: Rivals in Renaissance Venice" (*Times Literary Supplement,* May 27, 2009), p. 80.
36. Howard, *The Architectural History of Venice*, p. 78.
37. Van Akin Bard, *Christmas Story: John Ruskin's Venetian Letters of 1876–77* (Associated University Presses, London, 1990), p. 141.
38. Vircondelet, Alain, *Venice Art and Architecture* (Flammarion, Paris, 2006), p. 44.
39. Christopher Benfey, "Heaven and Earth" (Slate.com, 1997).
40. Malcolm Gladwell, *Outliers* (Little, Brown and Company, Boston, 2008), p. 93.
41. Gore Vidal, *Vidal in Venice* (Summit Books, New York, 1981), p. 95.
42. Giorgio Vasari, *The Lives of the Painters* (reprint, Oxford University Press, 1991), p. 94.
43. Mary McCarthy, *Venice Observed* (Harcourt, New York, 1963).
44. Bernard Berenson, *Italian Painters of the Renaissance* (Phaidon Press, London, 1952), p. 96.
45. James Ackerman, *Andrea Palladio* (Penguin Books, New York, 1983).
46. Nathaniel Kahn, *My Architect: A Son's Journey* (documentary film, 2003).
47. Vitruvius, *The Ten Books on Architecture,* trans. Morris Morgan (reprint, Harvard University Press, Cambridge, MA, 1914).

48. Witold Rybczynski, *The Perfect House: A Journey with the Renaissance Master Andrea Palladio* (Scribner, New York, 2002), p. 103.

49. Jack McLaughlin, *Jefferson and Monticello* (Henry Holt and Company, New York, 1990), p. 54.

50. Rybczynski, *The Perfect House: A Journey with the Renaissance Master Andrea Palladio.*

51. Alexander Herzen, *My Past and Thoughts*, trans. Constance Garnett (reprint by University of California Press, 1982).

52. Henry James, *The Italian Hours* (Houghton Mifflin, New York, 1909), p. 46.

All paintings collection of the artist except:

Title Page: Collection of David and Rosalee McCullough

p. 10 Private Collection

p. 20 Private Collection

p. 23 Susan Ennis

p. 24 Collection of Mary Burnham

p. 29 Collection of The Art Institute of Chicago

p. 34 Collection of The Museum of Fine Arts, Houston

p. 44 Christian Keesee

p. 60 Private Collection

p. 82 Collection of Oscar Shamamian and Llewellyn Sinkler

p. 85 Collection of George and Patsy Labalme

p. 90 Private Collection

p. 95 Mr. and Mrs. Ledlie Laughlin

p. 102 Institute of Classical Architecture

p. 105 Collection of Marshall Allan and Karen LaGatta

p. 112 Christian Keesee

ACKNOWLEDGMENTS

This book would not have been possible without the assistance of certain individuals who were generous with their time and advice. Special thanks goes to those who offered to read the manuscript, including the authors Judith Stonehill and Sidney Offit; Starling Lawrence, Senior Editor at W. W. Norton & Company; and Fred Hills, former Simon & Schuster editor. For their careful copyediting contributions, I thank Paula Cooper, Alex Griffith, and Gus Friedlander. I am grateful to George Labalme, John Hargraves, and David and Rosalee McCullough for their helpful suggestions early on; and to Jerry Kelly who encouraged the project and did a beautiful job designing it. Bill Zinsser offered ideas as to how to structure the book, Ralph Gardner, Jr. shared his valuable comments, and Peter Warner was instrumental as a liaison with the publisher. I thank David Godine for his enthusiasm for the project; Professor Rabb for his excellent scholarship and Simon Winchester for his impassioned insights; and my wife, Charlotte, for her sharp eye and careful consideration of each word.

Set in
Centaur types,
based on the types of
Nicolas Jenson, who printed in
Venice in the fifteenth century,
with Garamond italics.
Design by Jerry Kelly,
New York.

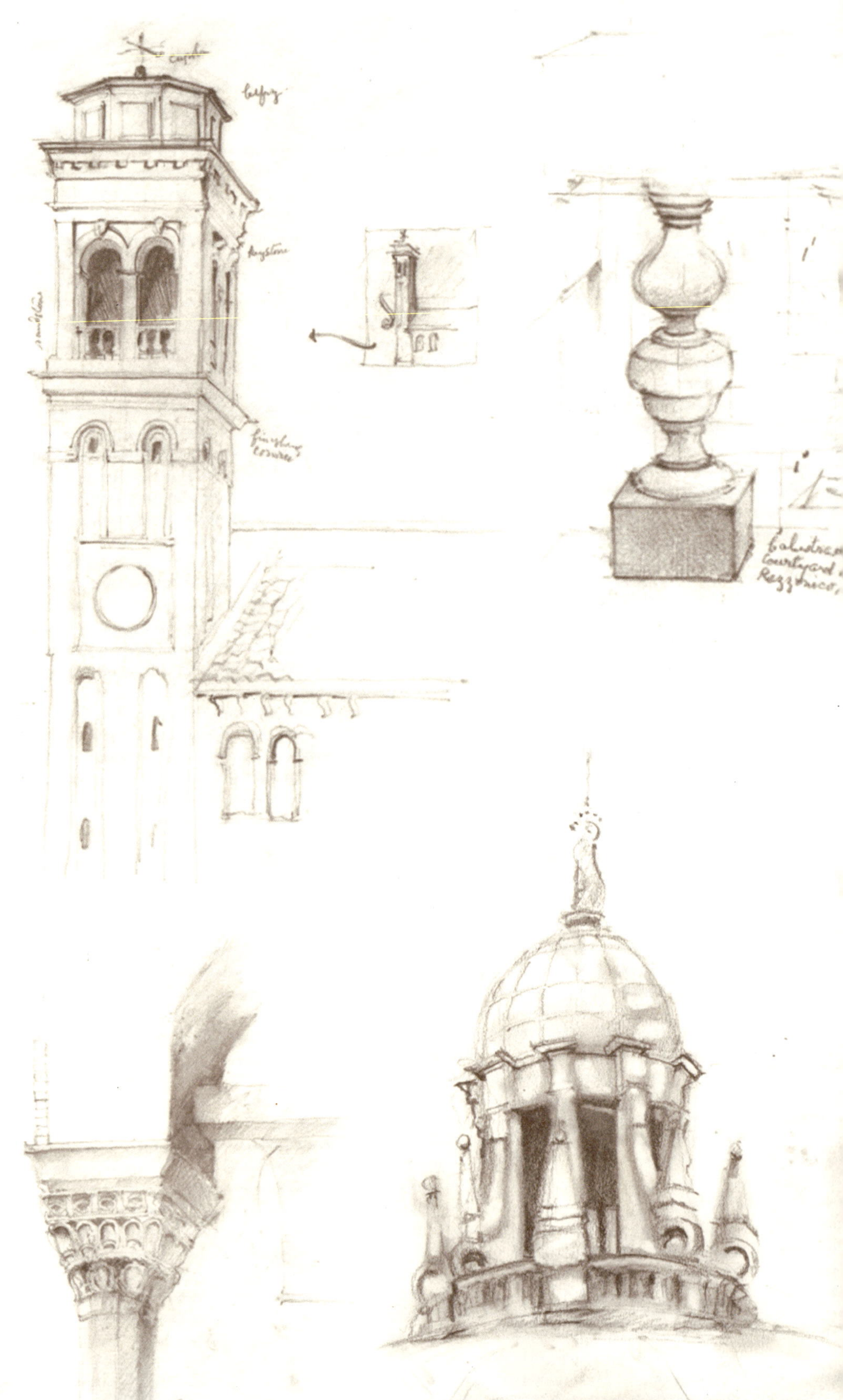
belfry
keystone